breaking through my limits

breaking through my limits

AN OLYMPIAN UNCOVERED

ALEXANDRA ORLANDO

B
BURMANBOOKS
.COM

Published by BurmanBooks Inc.
260 Queens Quay West
Suite 1102
Toronto, Ontario
Canada M5J 2N3

Interior design: Jack Steiner
Cover design: Diane Kolar
Cover photographs: Henrieta Haniskova
Editor: Drew Tapley

Distribution:
Innovative Logistics LLC
575 Prospect Street, Suite 301
Lakewood, NJ 08701

ISBN: 978-1-927005-02-6

For anyone who's ever felt like
they weren't good enough.

This is for you.

Contents

Acknowledgements

For every person you see that has achieved a piece of greatness in their lives, there are hundreds of people who helped them get there that you don't see. These are the people behind them every step of the way who gave their time, work and love, without wanting anything in return. They don't care about the spotlight or the glory. They care about you. They care about your dreams, and deeply believe that you can achieve them.

The amount of support I have received over the years from my family, friends, country, and even total strangers from all over the world, is truly humbling. I never believed it until I saw it with my own eyes: that who I was could affect people's lives. I had this gift that I could use to inspire others, and with that kind of power came strength.

Over the years I gave so many people the opportunity to give up on me. Some took it, but others never lost faith in what I could do. Even when I was so down, they were there. Every young gymnast who told me that they believed they didn't have to look a certain way because of what I had done; every friend who put up with my unreturned phone calls; every person who wanted the Olympics so badly for me—they empowered me to find myself and my potential. They helped me heal and somehow survive this crazy adventure, and find my next one.

Finally putting my story down on paper has been one of the most incredible experiences of my life. I couldn't have done this without my editor, Drew. Thank you for letting me use my voice, for giving me the chance to speak the words I have wanted to say for so long. You let me fight for things I wanted, and through shaping this book, you shaped me.

To my publisher, Sanjay, and BurmanBooks. Thank you for taking a chance on me, this ambitious girl who wanted to tell her story. You believed in me on a whim, and I see you as more than just my publisher, but my friend.

Thank you to those in the rhythmic gymnastics community across the world who appreciated that I was different, and who support this book. To the judges and coaches who fought for me, and to my coach Mimi for creating a champion. I wanted to be an Olympian, and you made it happen. It wasn't perfect, but we accomplished something that people only dream of. You pushed me, and I passed my limits. At our best, I felt as though I was flying; my mind and body on such an extreme high. It is something I don't know I'll ever feel again. Thank you for taking me there, for finding it inside of me.

To all my teammates over the years, I can't thank you enough for giving me the support I needed when I doubted myself. No one else will ever understand what we went through, but we will never be able to forget it. Each one of you stood beside me when things were crumbling, and you made me stronger.

To all the people who have told me that who I am has made them feel better about themselves, that my story helped them. You gave me the strength to write my biggest fears and secrets down on paper and publish them for the world to see. If you ever feel like you're nothing, remember my words, remember that being different is a strength. You are good enough.

To all my friends, you know who you are. I can't thank you enough for accepting me for who I am: A complete hurricane that falls off the face of the earth, horrible at keeping in touch at times, and too busy for my own good. You made me laugh when I hadn't smiled in weeks, helped me to see the good in my life no matter what I was going through. You love me for me, not what I accomplished, and I am forever grateful for that. I acknowledge that without the following people in my life, and many more, it may not have been possible to achieve all I have as an Olympic athlete. It would not have been possible to write this book:

Danielle, there are people in life that are true family, and you are one of them. You have a creativity and uniqueness that I have never seen before. A force to be reckoned with. Always on the same wavelength, we will be forever connected. Fifteen years as best friends; and here's to another fifteen by your side.

Mercy, your spirit is magical. You are hungry for life, for creativity, for a good cause, for a taste of the unexpected, and for adventure. You make me believe that anything is possible.

Rita, you have seen it all, witnessed my biggest accomplishments and failures: the heartbreak, the bad decisions, the growth. You have seen me morph into the woman I have become, and have always given me the love and support I needed when I felt unsteady on my own two feet.

Niki, you have always wanted the best for me, and kept me grounded over all these years. We can sit and talk for hours on end without once coming up for air. We're brutally honest and say what we mean because we care about each other like sisters.

Gaby, when I met you I was starting my new life, one without sport, without being the athlete. You brought me back to life into a world that I had always wanted to experience. Your energy and enthusiasm for everything and everyone around you is contagious.

Veronica, who would have thought that the quiet blonde that I stood next to every morning while getting my books out of my locker, would be one of my best friends ten years later. You're blunt and brilliant—the one I always turn to in order to knock some sense into me, which I desperately need sometimes.

Kyle, you respect me and always talked to me like I'm an adult, pushing me to think in ways I hadn't thought of before. You help me see new perspectives and learn about myself. Not only do you take care of me, but you take care of the person I love the most in this world: my sister. You're a constant source of love and support.

Mark, I'll always try and find someone to look at me, right through me, like you did. This book, this first step towards being honest with myself, has given me the strength to see the power you once had over me, and take it back. I learned the hard way that you can't always trust the people you fall for.

Eric, you have forever changed me and who I am. You made me feel something again. I hope deep down you think of me when the Bills are playing and you're wearing our jersey, or the millionth time Kings of Leon comes on your iPod. I wasn't ready to open myself up to someone again, but you got me there. Go explore, learn, free fall into the unknown, and I hope it takes you all over the world because that's where I see you.

Through all of this growing, my family has and always will be my greatest source of inspiration. They make me fearless. Each one of them has touched my life so deeply that they will never fully understand how much they mean to me. I will never be able to thank them for watching over me all these years and making my dream their dream. We always have each other to fall back on. It's in our blood. This is for you. Mia Famiglia.

Foreword

For those of you that often wondered what makes a champion, someone that excels beyond expectations, I encourage you to read this very personal and engaging book by Alexandra Orlando, one of Canada's most successful female athletes. I have had the good fortune of seeing "Alex" grow from an awkward but talented teenaged athlete into an inspirational young woman who shattered records around the world, always with grace, poise and humility.

Our Canadian amateur athletes are a special breed. After 20 years of involvement with them, I still wonder at their dedication, focus, determination and strength of character. None of them have unrealistic expectations of financial success from sport—quite the opposite. They all sacrifice for their sport, as do their families. Yet, this amazing cohort of young people from every part of Canada and from every different family background, have a common trait, a strong belief in their country, a desire to represent all of us well, and a determination to win medals not just for themselves, but also for Canada.

Alex has done a wonderful job in her book, bringing to life the very real struggles our athletes face on the road to elite level international competition and the winners' podium. Most of us only see the magical moment of triumph on our TV screens. Alex's book tells the story of the arduous journey to get there, the pain and sacrifice, the many losses and near wins that precede great victory, and yes, the thrill of success.

Perhaps the body of an elite level athlete is a gift, but I can assure you that the mind, skill and character of a champion is not a genetic fluke, it is the years in the pursuit of excellence and dogged determination that transforms the gift and propels them to heights we can only marvel at. I claim perspective on athletes despite never being one. I've had the benefit of working with them from several vantage points, and they continue to inspire me. Whether as head of an organizing committee, head of a major sponsor, or chair of a fundraising group, our athletes have never disappointed me or let me down. In those 20 years I've seen many win, far more lose, but every one of them gave everything they had, for themselves, their families, their supporters and their country.

Alex's book is a poignant story of an athlete coming of age, navigating not only the turmoil of youth, but also the pressure of competition and the path to international gold medals. I have watched Alex compete many times in many countries, but my fondest and most telling memory was off the field of play. An important part of sport is raising funds so that our athletes can train and compete. Government grants cover a fraction of the costs. As an advocate for our athletes, I've never been bashful about asking the public and private sector for money to support our athletes. I always brought along my secret weapon, the athletes themselves. They are so gifted, so compelling, that potential sponsors and supporters were generally transfixed by their message, none more so than Alex.

Alex is an inspirational speaker, connecting with the many audiences we spoke to. She gave of her time unstintingly despite a hectic schedule of school, training, and competition. At one such event, leading up to the 2006 Melbourne Commonwealth Games, she casually leaned over to me just before I went up to speak, and told me she was going to win 5 gold medals in Australia. It wasn't boastful or bravado, and not a hint of ego, it was a statement pure and simple, delivered with her usual soft voice and engaging smile. I dutifully reported that conversation to our potential sponsors. Read her book, and find out how that promise turned out!

That was many years and events ago. Alex has grown into an inspiring and accomplished young woman, one of our most successful athletes, and she continues to support our athletes after retiring from competition. I recommend her book to you, you will find it touching, truthful and compelling, an excellent insight into the making of a champion, told by a real person with humour, humility and compassion.

George Heller
Chair of the Commonwealth Games Foundation
Former CEO & President of the Hudson's Bay Company

Prologue

Long before "gymnast" was officially attached to the end of my name, I was just Alex.

I can barely remember her now, what she felt like, who she was. A memory, a life so deep into my past it's been washed away as if it never existed. I sit at the kitchen table now, close my eyes and imagine her then. A life she had only just begun living, a world she only saw in her dreams. That little girl would single-handedly change the course of her family's life with the decisions she made and the goals she set for herself. No one saw it coming.

There are moments when time seems to stand still, not for long, but long enough to catch a glimpse of the people buzzing around you. You're the one in slow motion. Leaning over the kitchen counter reading or writing, I'm always in someone's way. My father's in the fridge searching for something to satisfy his appetite before dinner, of course; and my mother is frustrated that we're in her domain, while my sister is talking so loud the room vibrates. Food and dishes litter the counters, and it seems like we make and eat food simultaneously sometimes. Music is blaring and my nonna (grandmother) is attempting to add things to my mother's concoction, which is never a good idea. The room comes to life. I close my eyes and feel ten again, at the same table in the same room. But so much has happened in my short lifetime that I don't believe I could be back there again. It was so long ago that I lived under this roof, back to a time and to a life that seems like a distant dream to me now.

This house where it all began has scattered memories and pieces of a past that once consumed us. You can walk through and catch a glimpse of a medal hiding under a pile of papers, or a framed picture of my former life. Our former life, I should say. Alex in Bulgaria, Alex in France, Spain, Brazil, China.... It was nothing out of the ordinary to see half-filled suitcases in the hallways or flight itineraries taped to the fridge. My childhood room is a shrine to athletics. There are photo albums under the coffee table of Alex the Athlete, Alex the Gymnast. It's hard to believe I even existed out of the gym. There are hardly any photos of me that aren't related to sport. My older sister Victoria has boxes documenting her first steps, her first dance, and every family event where my mom could play dress-up with her. When I think of my big sis as a kid, she is an Orlando. We're both all sass and a little bit of trouble. But for anyone who has met us, that's a given.

My photos consist of a little girl in a bun and pink velvet catsuits, the occasional tracksuit, and a million gymnastic poses. You can feel my energy bursting out of the photographs, my big smile and buckteeth glistening, my eyes taking charge. I was an infectious bundle of something, a spunky kid with this larger than life persona; a brat, a drama queen, and a hilariously funny and entertaining spitfire. I was a handful and always will be. It's in my nature.

Every single person in this kitchen was affected by who I had become. I'll have to live with that for the rest of my life. They took it all—the good, the bad, and the horribly ugly. Never a dull moment. And not once did they complain. For years we never went on a family vacation as I could never get any time off training. My mom had to shuttle my teammates and I back and forth to the gym, feed me, and make sure I pulled through those exhausted mornings when I couldn't drag myself out of bed. Without her it would have all fallen apart. I was too young to do it alone, and my mom was my agent, by my side to guide me, in front to protect me, and behind me to help me climb that hill. We were inseparable for so many years, our lives intertwined and so tightly woven that she knew everything, all the time. It became her full-time job, and she naturally filled the role, never once doubting why she was devoting her life to this. She gave up her time so selflessly and put her nerves on the line, all for me. When you're younger you have no idea what that means, what kinds of sacrifices people make for you. You can't even fathom what they give up for your dreams, not theirs, and what they battle for you, and only you. She gave up not only her time, but a life she may have wanted and a break to relax that she never got. It is because of her that we have the photos that adorn the hallways. It is because of her willingness to make me happy that I can say, "I'm an Olympian". It is because of her that our family has stayed together through those rough times when you don't think you'll be able to recover.

A glimpse into our lives is easy enough. Just step inside our kitchen and you'll find us—the real Orlandos. The commotion inside looks confusing, almost alarming with heated body language. But take a closer look and you'll see that we're not yelling or mad at all. Over the top, exaggerated and loud, the Orlando household has always been one full of surprises. Look again, closer this time, and the frail older woman with fiery red hair is my nonna, Flora. You can tell that there's a story behind her eyes, a sadness that only a widow would recognize, the tiredness of a woman who won't give up. When she smiles, it looks familiar, like a Mona Lisa.

The woman with the killer haircut and the stylish clothes, who never sits down—that's my mother, Marisa. The Energizer Bunny that takes care of everyone but herself. This is her domain. She controls the room, jumping between the stove, the grill, the fridge and the sink… and we all just get in her way. She smiles at our laughter, shakes her head at our stupidity, and sighs when we tease her, and even worse when we imitate her. She's an open book, and even from afar you can see how we all abuse her good heart.

The tanned, incredibly jacked guy with a drink in his hand is my father, Paul, or "Paully" in a New York accent, as we know him. Standing next to him or even from a house's length away, there is no mistaking that this man is larger than life. People who don't even know him, gravitate to him. The wild way he tells stories and the strong drinks he mixes, this "25-year-old" keeps getting younger and younger. He's a magnet, and you're mesmerized by him no matter how many times you might have heard the same story.

You can tell that the beautiful girl sitting beside him marches to her own beat. With an edgy, curly haircut, and skin draped with jewellery, she captures the attention of everyone in the room. You couldn't miss this one. That's my older sister, Victoria, the girl I would've died to be for so many years. We still argue over our seat at the table and about cutting each other off when trying to tell a story. She is louder than my father, if you can believe it, learned from the best; and she brings our family together. She's a diva and a hippie at heart. Every time she rolls her eyes, you know she means business.

Sitting there, more often than not quietly, is a young man who cannot possibly be related to these crazy people. Caucasian, clean cut with a smirk on his face, he must have been dragged into this mess. It's my brother-in-law, Kyle. The way he looks at my sister gives it away, they must be in love. I could only wish for someone to look at me like that one day. Soaking it all in, he seems amused and intrigued. Over the past ten years you'd think he'd get tired of us. He's a Thunder Bay boy stuck in a Sicilian soap opera. It doesn't get any better than that.

And then there's a young woman leaning on the table, legs crossed underneath her, perched like a cat ready to pounce. She's constantly playing with her long black hair, and you can't seem to figure this one out. She's a mystery, jumping in enthusiastically to a conversation one second, only to sink into her chair with stubborn pursed lips the next. She barely sips her vino, but lovingly rests her head on Victoria's shoulder or messes up Marisa's hair. There's pain there, but fire. A light inside of her desperately trying to shine. She'll find her way; you can feel it in your bones.

Long before sport and before gymnastics, I think we were a normal family once. I actually don't remember a time when someone would describe us as normal. The beauty of my family and why we are so connected is that we're not afraid of fighting, of saying whatever we want and letting things get heated. We make fun of each other, we always want to have a good time, and we fill our house with music. It's a vibe, a frequency that hits you right in the face when you walk in the door. It is warm and inviting, everyone is welcome here. They all have such an incredible way of making you feel like you belong. In this crazy, overloaded, overwhelming world, I am grateful to come home to something real, something beautiful, something we take for granted when we shouldn't.

Fifteen years we've been under the same roof, and if only these walls could talk. The scenes it's seen, the words it's heard, the tears that we tried to hide. This house knows us better than we know ourselves. All the rolled eyes, the looks shot across the room and the quiet days where you could be sad when no one was watching. Even through the hard times, the amount of joy that soaked into the very foundations of the house, the beams that hold it all together, kept us standing tall. The laughter, storytelling and family time that I could always count on made navigating the last couple of years actually possible. Without them by my side, I never would have had the life that I did. If these walls could talk, they would say that we are people that become our best selves when we're around each other. We are a family that thrives on good music, good food, good company and good times. We make fun of each other and yell. We dance in the middle of our living room and on tables. We pour wine like we pour out our hearts to the ones we love. We will protect each other no matter what, blood is thicker than water. I would go to the end of the earth and back for any one of them. They are my base, and they make me who I am. We worry about each other, we feel each other's pain, and we will always be there for one another no matter what.

We are not a perfect family, but we are perfect to me. I wouldn't change one thing about us for the world. In every flaw there is a positive, in every weakness there is a silent strength. We are continuously learning from each other. We are living.

Sitting around our kitchen table, we learn, we grow, we cry, we hate. We realize who we are and what we couldn't live without: the secrets, the shame, the joys, the triumphs, and the little moments where our love is the strongest. This table holds our weight, like a rock, unwavering no matter how rough the storm. The cold marble that is stained with our tears is a part of us. It remembers the broken glasses and late night rendezvous. It remembers the people that it has touched, and their stories. There's no escaping it.

Over the years I have transformed into the woman I am today, all in front of their eyes. Phase by phase they have seen me fall, dust myself off and get back up again. Fall and stay down, suffocating. Drowning, but finding air to breathe. Fall, get back up and learn from my mistakes, find my footing, climb higher, push through and feel the light shine on my face.

They were there when I was that little gymnast who didn't know who she was, and the tomboy that fought off any boy who made fun of her sport. They were there when I started travelling all over the world and found myself Canadian National Champion at thirteen, and when I missed qualifying for the Olympics. They were there when my world came crashing down all around me, when I lost myself. They were there when I broke a World Record, and when I fell in love. They were there when I got my heart broken, and when I finally marched into the Olympic stadium behind the Canadian flag.

They were there when I retired and gave it all up. They were there when I found myself.

I couldn't tell you how I dragged myself out of bed some days

How I begged and pleaded with that voice inside my head

The exhaustion consumed me

I could feel the heaviness in my heart

But it's just one more day

You can get through this, you're stronger than this

Try a little harder girl, there's no excuses now

What's the matter with you?

Get up now she said, it's time to go now she said

How I dreaded those words

Another day, another day of the unexpected

Would I make it through? I never knew

What's the matter with you?

If you don't want to be here, it's too late for that, you have to

They're all watching you, counting on you

Try a little harder girl, there's no excuses now

You wanted this remember

No turning back

Just get through today and forget about tomorrow

Counting only makes the days seem longer

breaking
through
my limits

Chapter 1:
Alex the Gymnast

From the beginning I was just a girl that loved to play sports, and was an extremely competitive little thing. I played it all, and wanted to win. Even a game of soccer or baseball with the boys at recess became the World Cup or the World Series. And I was the worst sore loser, always wanting to be the best, not settling for anything less. I would practice over and over again to be better the next time, to come out on top. I was fast. Not the most technically skilled, but the one that tried the hardest. There's something to be said for those kids that may not be a natural, but work harder than any of their teammates. These are the ones that come in early and run drills, and keep pushing and pushing themselves. They listen to their coaches, watch others, learn, and make a conscious effort to get better, to prove to themselves that they can do it. They are the ones with heart. When I was younger, I never really understood that expression. We all have heart, we all show up to play and be a part of a team. What did that mean?

When I went from just playing sports to starting a career as a Canadian athlete, I began to realize just what it took to be an athlete and compete for your country. This was the heart that everyone was talking about, the heart that you needed to make it.

It was a fluke that I even found rhythmic gymnastics to begin with, which was the most obscure, unpopular, least respected sport in North America. I was five years old, and after getting delicately kicked out of ballet lessons for being too rambunctious, it was recommended that I try this thing called "rhythmic". My parents had never heard of it before. They had played traditional sports.

My dad grew up playing baseball in the Bronx. They weren't used to anything like this, but we found a small club in Toronto, one of the first ones in the city, and thought we'd give it a try. Victoria got roped into trying it as well.

We would go to Saturday morning classes at a public school, squeeze into little blue bodysuits, and run around for a few hours. This was my first exposure to the sport, and I was hooked. It was the most challenging thing I had ever tried. Rhythmic gymnastics is a combination of acrobatics, gymnastics, dance, ballet, and Cirque de Soleil skills. There are five different apparatus: rope, hoop, ball, clubs, and ribbon. Not only do you have to master how to handle each one, but also learn four different body techniques and perform it all simultaneously and effortlessly. Flexibilities, balances, turns and jumps are the main components, and take years to perfect and hone. There are moves you will never master, and ways of contorting your body that only a select few individuals can achieve. Each body group has dozens of elements for all different levels that each gymnast works her way through; some never being attempted. The sheer skill and ability to execute elements depends on your natural flexibility, over extension, balance, coordination, and fearlessness. This is a sport that is all about repetition. Doing one thing over and over and over, waking up the next day bruised, cut and sore, and doing it again, re-opening the burns and scabs—repeating it until you get it, and then get it again. Not only are you meant to perform flawlessly, but you must squeeze all your elements into a minute and a half that flows to a piece of instrumental music with ease. Masking the intense power, strength and energy with beauty and grace is the name of the game, and probably the hardest part of the sport. It is meant to look easy. This is what you work endless hours in the gym to achieve, to be able to shut your eyes and move your body with an almost innate precision, knowing exactly how to move your feet to a rhythm, upside down, bent in half on the floor with a ball balanced in your back. It's about feeling the music from within, and being able to check your nerves at the door and perform in front of a firing squad of judges, scrutinizing your every move, breath and finger placement. When I was five, I just wanted to have fun doing something I thought would be easy. Rhythmic definitely wasn't this. My face would go beet red as I stood on my tiptoes trying to make a perfect set of spirals with a ribbon that was six metres long, and which shouldn't touch the floor. My arm muscles would give out after ten seconds. Who knew the amount of energy that went into such a simple-looking thing? That's what drew me in: that I couldn't do something I thought I could. To master this skill was such a big feat, such an accomplishment, that it couldn't compare to scoring a goal at soccer or running on a track. For me, this was my Everest, and I felt like that every single day for the next seventeen years of my life—striving for perfection, knowing that you could always be better, you could always work harder, and you could always take yourself further.

Ever since the beginning, rope has always been my nemesis. It's a thinner, heavier skipping rope intricately woven to be a lean, mean fighting machine. To get a good grip on it you tie two knots at the ends and burn off the edges so it doesn't fray. Every gymnast has their own way of tying the ends to fit with their hands. It's all about feel. You become hyper aware of your body through working with each apparatus that it's almost a sixth sense. My rope and I never got along. It whipped me, gave me burns and scars, and it took years for me to get a feel for her. She had a mind of her own in a sport where you need to be in control every single second. Rope skills are fast and complicated, and the shapes you make need to be precise and sharp. When throwing it up in the air you need to know that the knots are coming down perfectly into your hands, and it needs to be perfect at all times.

Jumps are the main body component that aligns with the rope event. Every routine is a minute and a half, and within that there are requirements for every athlete, just like figure skating. Every few years the code of points changes, and the number of elements goes up or down depending on whether the apparatus skills increase. Some years there is more focus on the artistic component of the sport, the music, the flow, and tricks with the apparatus;

and there are bonus points for athletes who try incredibly difficult skills. Other years it's difficulty based, with more emphasis on body elements and how many high level jumps you can fit into the time limit. Gymnasts constantly have to adapt and transform their skills and abilities. The best girls in the world are the ones that can do it all, that have the technical and the artistic side, the power and the grace.

Jumps are the most physically demanding of the body groups. You have to jump high and lightly. It's more than just doing the splits in the air. There are jumps where you completely bend in half while taking flight, some that involve turning, and some where you even lose sight of the ground and are contorting your body in ways that you never thought possible. You have to use the momentum of your takeoff and your arms to lift you up, and another technique to guide you through a proper landing. There are jumps where you switch your legs into positions in the air within milliseconds, and perform these two or three times in a row. You can't forget the apparatus either, which has to be constantly moving, and most of the time you are trying to throw it up twenty feet in the air or catch it while you're mid-jump.

Hoop was always my favourite. It has similar characteristics to a hula hoop, but it definitely isn't one. It's thicker and heavier, made of a special kind of plastic that is malleable but firm. The way it moves on your hands or rotates in the air depends on its shape, and to keep it in good shape and not warped is always a challenge. Your hoop should come up to your hip bone, but mine was always smaller, which meant it was faster, and I could manipulate it better. With most apparatus there are planes that you have to keep it rotating on for good technique. But trying to teach someone how to rotate a hoop on their hand can take months, which is the most basic move. It came naturally to me, and I was able to get a feel for it early on, being able to toss it up in the air and perform two or three somersaults underneath it, catching it in my legs on the floor, or behind my back. There are so many interesting skills you can come up with, and I used to count down the days till the summer when I could just play around with it and come up with new ways of throwing it up in the air or catching it. The sky is the limit. You can use your feet, your hands, your neck; throw it in any direction, behind your back, in the middle of an acrobatic element or jump. Hoop combines all the different body groups, and means you can pick and choose your best from the jumps, turns, balances and flexibilities category. It was always my time to show off, and it was the one apparatus that never really made me nervous when I was compcting. Call it my lucky charm, but it calmed my nerves and set my confidence high. I could always rely on it to bring me up if I was having a particularly hard day at the gym (most of the time anyways). We had the occasional fights where it didn't want to cooperate with me, it was in a mood… but I always forgave him.

The ball is always heavier than people think, made of a thick plastic in all different colours and styles to match your personality or the theme of the routine. Ball was always my most emotional routine: The slower, dramatic event to showcase my expression as a dancer, which is my other passion. The whole focus of ball is to make it seem like it's an extension of your body, that it flows smoothly from hand to hand and all over your body. When you throw it up in the air, that's the only time it leaves the touch of your skin. As I got older, it was the most sensual, the most rhythmic of apparatus. It was beautiful if executed perfectly; a story being told in every step, every wave and shape your body made. There was something about it. It was as if the stadium would get so quiet all you could hear was the wind you were making with your movements. The ball was silent, rolling over the contours you made with your body, a mysterious love affair. As I changed as a person, my performances grew with me. My routines expressed a new part of me, a more emotional and more mature Alex. As I became a woman, exploring these newfound feelings through music and movement was liberating.

The clubs are always the hardest apparatus to explain to people who haven't stepped foot anywhere near the world of gymnastics.

Clubs are long, hard and solid plastic batons that when held in your hand come up just past your elbows. They have a small ball on one end to hold in between your thumb and pointer finger, and a larger head that has always reminded me of a tulip. You have to see them to fully understand what they are; but they are definitely the most vicious, cruel apparatus of them all. When you're younger there's no mercy, and you learn very quickly not to let yourself bend your arms when working with them because you think that will be easier. When rotating these nunchucks in your hands, one bent elbow can send you to the hospital with a broken nose. I can't count the bruises, bumps and black eyes that they've given me. You have to build up calluses to handle them, and when you're first learning, your hands shake a little when you pull them out of your gym bag. Your shins brace themselves for what's to come. Clubs are the most difficult apparatus to master, and when I talk about being fearless, this is where it comes in. You have to throw both up in the air, rotating perfectly beside each other in alignment, attempting to catch them out of your vision or with other parts of your body. Sprained and broken fingers become the norm. I even knew of a girl that looked up and got hit right in the mouth, chipping her front teeth.

The main body element is balances, which are meant to slow you down so you can rotate the clubs and keep them moving constantly. Balances can consist of any shape you can imagine, like holding your leg up by your head with no help from your hands, or your body leaned forward with one of your legs straight up behind you, or even bending yourself into a straight line while holding on to one of your ankles from behind. Whatever shape you're in, a balance is only a balance if you're standing on the ball of your foot, up on your tiptoes, and you freeze in that pose for at least three seconds. It's the longest three seconds of your life, clenching every single muscle, willing yourself to hold it. Of course, this is also while you are performing some sort of technique with the clubs in whatever hand you have free. The sound you would always try and avoid was the crashing weight of one of them hitting the floor. That sound always seemed to reverberate off the floor and into every room of the stadium, letting all your competitors know you just opened up a chance for them to knock you right out of medal contention.

Of all the apparatus, ribbon was what I was known for. It was the most unpredictable apparatus, the one that gave everyone problems, even the world champions. She's fickle, but I had learned to read her signals and get into her head. She's six meters of silk ribbon, a few inches thick, which could never stop moving, hit the floor or your body. The ribbon was attached to a long, thin plastic stick that had a metal swivel to hold the two pieces together. Not only did it have to be constantly moving, but in shapes that were sharp, crisp and noticeable to all judges. Spirals were to be small and tight, every movement was to have a purpose, and every shape had to have meaning. When thrown in the air, it needed to create a cascading arch that seemed to float through the air. Not always my best event, but I grew into it, and it became my thing. I was able to turn like no one else, and I was fast, so much faster than my competitors. I would fly around the carpet dazzling the judges with the amount of rotations I performed and the technique I had. I rarely had a problem with ribbon, it was organic to me, something that I took pride in. I was the most comfortable and the most myself out there, and ribbon became a part of my persona as a gymnast. My ribbon routines were known worldwide. It became a must-see—my claim to fame.

As I try and describe my sport in words, it doesn't do it justice. I shut my eyes and see the girls I worshipped for so many years: the Eastern European world champions. These are athletes who seemed to do the impossible, who could connect with an audience across the world on a small television in a basement somewhere. I was a little girl sitting in a bodysuit, pointing her toes and watching these beautiful women perform. It's not dance. It's not acrobatics. It's not a circus act. It's its own creation. A performance sport. Rhythmic gymnastics embodies the idea that every athlete and coach could take their imagination to the limit and play with the body to create something unbelievable. It was something that came from inside of you.

When I was younger, no one understood why I would want to give up soccer and track to do gymnastics. I was teased mercilessly at the time from boys who thought I was a stupid girl playing with a stick and a ribbon. But I loved it. That was all my parents needed to hear. My sister gave it up, not her thing. But for the first time it was my thing. I wasn't copying her, or ending up in classes because she had already done them first and it was an easy carpool commute for my mom. No, this was all mine. I have never worked harder in my life than I did those first, early years of competing. I went from recreational Saturday morning classes to training three times a week, and then six times a week in what seemed like only a few months. It all happened so quickly.

I started at a small club, one of the few clubs in Toronto at the time, and was surrounded by Eastern European culture and mannerisms. Estonian and Russian became the two languages I came to recognize very early on. I would race out of the car to get to the gym when my mom dropped me off for practice. My recreational coaches knew that I had the potential to start competing soon. I was only seven years old, but they could tell. I'll never forget when the day of "just doing it for fun" changed into something more serious. The feel in the gym was different, and I was scared. I remember holding my mom's hand as we walked into this new gym to meet my new competitive coach for the first time. It was in an old warehouse on Eastern Avenue where they filmed movies. At four stories high, the ceiling seemed to go on forever and ever. The gym could fit two full size competition carpets in it, and had a viewing area on the second floor for parents. There were change rooms and a carpeted space for ballet up on the third floor. Looking all around me, my eyes feasted on all the small details: the gym bags littering the floors, the ballet teacher's stern voice, and the faint sounds of piano music echoing down from some other room, some other world. My eyes were open wide, and couldn't take it all in. And then there was my coach, the Russian princess.

She barely spoke any English then, but came over to us as bubbly as she still is today with her long blonde hair, heels and lipstick. She was something out of a television show, and I remember thinking that she couldn't possibly be real. I let go of my mother's hand as she wanted to take a good look at me, a closer look. Right there she pulled down my pants to see my body in my gym suit. I think my mother was in shock, completely frozen to the spot. She twirled me around. I had passed the inspection, except that I needed to grow my hair. "Young gymnasts do not have hair like boy," she would say, and shake her head. And we did whatever she said. I started growing out my hair and coming three times a week. She was going to make me ready to compete. And did she ever.

This was a whole new world. The girls were competitive and catty. We fought for our coach's attention, always wanting to be the star. We were such a handful, so young and full of energy, moody and emotional. There were days when girls would sit and cry because they couldn't do something or didn't want to do it. She would yell, but only for a few minutes. She could be serious one moment and laughing and joking around with us the next, always finding that balance. I loved her. We trained on the older carpet beside the national level girls, who seemed larger than life to me once upon a time. But their coach was terrifying. She sat on the other side of the carpet so we didn't see her… but we could hear her! She had peroxide blonde hair, straight as nails with black roots. She only wore black, and these big stiletto boots. Her eyes were catlike and dark, haunting almost. She wasn't Russian, she was Bulgarian, and she couldn't have been more different to my coach. This woman, this woman that I would think of as a mother in years to come, could make the hair stand up on the back of your neck when she stared you down. She could make your knees shake, and the thought of that shrill voice as she trained our future Olympians can still wake me up from even the deepest of sleeps.

Here I was in this gym, this little thing getting ready to compete provincially for the first time, standing next to the beautiful and strong soon-to-be Canadian Olympian, Camille

Martens. She was a goddess to me. So strong, fast and passionate. I could feel her from a mile away, the wind she created as she hit every movement. It was with every ounce of her energy that she did everything. Every raise of her arm or arch of her back, her energy was incredible. You couldn't take your eyes off her. She was pushed and pushed, but she never broke. Camille was a machine in my eyes, and everything I wanted to be. Her coach told her to do something a hundred times, because maybe then she'd get it right. Camille didn't even blink an eye, but moved to the side of the carpet and repeated this skill over and over until she got it right a hundred times. I'll never forget her for the rest of my life: the sheer determination and unwillingness to give up. She left me in awe. I never looked up to any of the other national level girls like I did Camille. She was different. She had something that moved her from deep within herself that kept her going. I liked to think that I had that in me too. She always called me a street fighter, a little ball of fire. I wanted to be just like her.

I was lucky to have my provincial coach for two whole years before I was ready to go national. She nurtured me and gave me the tools I needed to succeed, and those first competitions were the most exhilarating moments of my young, little life. I loved to compete, and it showed. I don't remember being too nervous, more anxious to show off my routine that I had been working on for months. I felt calm with her standing behind me, hands on my shoulders, and she would whisper things in my ear, words of encouragement, things to remember. I would take it in and look at the judges and the crowd of people watching, and I waited for it to be my turn out there. Waves of excitement would come over me. Those first two years I was just getting my feet wet, realizing what it felt like not to win, to see some other girl come ahead of me, and to stare at my competition and feel the envy with a silver medal hanging around my neck. I was never the best, but always just so close with little mistakes that gave the others a chance to slide in front of me. Once I got a little taste of the top of the podium though, I wouldn't settle for anything less. I had no idea how competitive I could be. I remember strutting around the gym with my team, and we were so proud of our club and our little group. We stuck to ourselves and thought we were the coolest girls there, in head-to-toe velvet catsuits. I grew out of that phase quickly, thank God.

The next year I was actually known as being a pretty serious contender for provincial champion, and got a good dose of my own medicine when I didn't handle the pressure. It was provincials, and I remember everyone coming from the practice gym to watch me, to watch what I would do out there. This was one of the first times that I would let the nerves get to me, but it wouldn't be the last time. It was humbling to bite my tongue and stand off the podium, watching the silky ribbon hang from someone else's neck. I congratulated them and then sat in the car and cried all the way home. It was a slap in the face. The disappointment was brutal. I still had a long way to go, but I knew that my parents and my coach believed in me. My coach knew what was in store for me over the next few years, and it was that summer that she broke the news to me that I should go national. I remember her talking with my mom and explaining what that would mean, how many more days of training it would be, the extra hours in the gym and how much more it would cost them. My mom took it all in, and even though it wouldn't be easy, a burden more than anything else, she asked me what I wanted to do. I didn't know where it would take me, I had no idea what kind of road this would lead me down, but I knew that I wanted to get better. I wanted to keep doing gymnastics, and if I had the potential to move to the next level, then I would do it. My parents always just wanted me to be happy, and I am so grateful for that because I know not all athletes have that kind of support system. It's not just one person's sacrifice, it's a handful. When I began training every day except Saturday, it began to consume us. My sister still thought of me as a little brat, and probably welcomed me being out of the house every night. My mom became my permanent chauffeur. Forget dinners together, homework before 8:30 p.m., and any other sports. They forgot to mention one thing. I was going to be training with the national girls now... and with their coach.

My heart dropped. I gulped back a lump in my throat as I was walked over to this coach that I was so terrified of. She stood directly over me, looking down at me with those eyes of hers, and I could smell the smoke on her fingers. She smirked, speaking to me through her eyes, like an enchanted snake. She was otherworldly. I held her gaze, head tilted upwards, not daring to disrespect her in any way; and she looked me up and down and told me to go warm up with the others. I ran over there, away from my former coach and into my new life on the other side of the gym. This carpet was so much nicer than the one I used to train on, and we had mirrors lining the back of the wall with ballet bars. There were ten or twelve of us at this time, all national level, and I fell right into place where I was supposed to. I was the youngest, so I did everything first, including getting their apparatus and doing whatever they said. It was a hierarchy, and even then I understood that you just do what you're told. These girls were older, wiser, and more experienced. I was going to learn so much from them, and I did. I looked at my old group of teammates differently now, but I never stopped wishing I could still work with my first coach. She taught me the basics, the fundamentals; and she made me fall in love with the sport. No one else can take credit for that.

Working on this side of the gym was a whole other ball game. You never knew what to expect every time you stepped foot on the carpet, or what kind of mood my coach would be in that day. My mom got into the habit of picking her up from the subway with my teammates in tow, and she drove us all to training each day. I'm not quite sure how she fell into this role, but she would never refuse to help someone. My mother goes out of her way to help people regardless of whether it's an annoyance to her. She realized this meant something to me, and she wanted to be a part of it. These car rides, the thirty minutes it took to battle downtown Toronto traffic and the Don Valley Parkway, was our time to see our coach outside of the gym. She was surprisingly normal, hilarious in fact. With her larger than life, over the top personality and thick Bulgarian accent, she would tell wild stories and talk and talk. My mother would take it all in, nodding and agreeing with her complaints about her salary, her life, whatever it was that day she wanted to vent about. But she always looked back and smiled at me, with that huge grin. "Right Alex?" she would ask when she talked about how many more hours I needed to be in the gym or the types of competitions I needed to go to. She had all these big plans for me, for all of us. From all the chaos and craziness that would come of our relationship with her, she cared about us. We were her babies. I never expected to get as close to her as I did. I would do anything for her. When it was my turn to get new routines from her in the summer of my first year as a national novice, competing against young girls across the country, I was beyond nervous. I saw how she made other routines, how she moved to the music and we were supposed to imitate her. What if I couldn't do it? What if I froze in front of her? The very thought of it kept me up at night. And then my time finally came. She played the music over and over on our little, broken ghetto blaster, slamming in tape after tape trying to find the right music, the right cut of the music for me. There were no CDs then, it was all cassettes. The quality was scratchy and horrible, but we didn't have any better. She would finally come to one and would look at me. At first her face was completely stern, and then with a smile she would tell me to go get my apparatus.

She was a wild woman. Her imagination was unlike anyone's I had ever known. She would have an image, a movement in her head, and try and bring it to life with your body. Your arms, your legs. I would keep moving constantly to try and figure out what was going on in her head, what she wanted. When you got it, you better not forget what you just did. Hours and hours we would work together, and she would get frustrated with me when I didn't know what she was talking about or couldn't do something. Sweat would pour down my face and back. My back wasn't as flexible as it is now, and that was her biggest problem with me. I would try skills I've never done before, and fall on my face—all to please, all to create something beautiful. It was a work of art, a living, breathing statue moving through a painting. I wish someone had filmed us working together one day because she brought out every ounce of my being. Even at age ten or twelve, I found emotions inside of me that came alive. I was on fire, and she lapped it up and loved it. I had "gypsy blood," she used to say, with "those gypsy eyes like I could kill someone". There was a power growing inside of me then that I didn't realize, but she had tapped into it somehow, and I will never forget that. Maybe a different club, a different coach, a different path, and I never would have found it. So I will always thank her.

Those years I was attached at her hip. I wanted her attention, all of it, and I wouldn't stop working in the gym, not to talk nor to fool around. I wanted her to think I was special, that I was different from all of them, and to compare me to the older ones and see that I could go all the way, to be number one like one of her older girls who was senior level, the highest you can go, and an Olympic contender. She was worked with and praised the most. We were all such little girls who just wanted her love and approval. I didn't know it then, I didn't want to see it maybe, but it was consuming her, the pressure to have a national champion, for her girls to win and to be the best. I was national novice champion by then. She had the junior champion, but senior was still out of her grasp, and I think it secretly must of driven her insane. She would be so disgusted with us when we weren't training well, and would throw our music tapes or pens at us. I remember her storming after me one day in her outdoor shoes, coming onto the carpet to stand over me and yell. I felt two feet tall with her blonde hair hanging over my face. Some called our relationship crazy, but I called her my second mom. She was a mad genius, misunderstood, and in the end—she just lost it. She was so talented, but let it go to waste. The pressure, the stress, the expectations, I don't think we'll ever know. Maybe she cared too much, but that one summer it all fell apart. My parents didn't want me to head to South Africa for a training camp with some of the girls, so I stayed back that one time. Good thing I did. I didn't witness what they did, experience what they experienced. I could never say if she hit her. I wasn't there, but I know what I heard.

When everyone came back to the gym, things were different. Girls quit, they didn't want to work with her, and it was as if there was some secret that I didn't know. I was confused. And then the lawsuits came, the trial, the testimonies. I was only twelve, so why did I have to testify without my mom? Her lawyer made me sit directly in front of her as I cried. She was my second mother, and I didn't know what was happening. I answered all their questions, all their little games and traps they tried to get me to fall into. I just told the truth. I know what I saw, how we worked every day, and I didn't think anything of it. I never wanted to betray her, and would never have done that. She smiled at me, her eyes brimming with tears as I spoke, explaining how I felt about her, how much I cared for her. She never touched me, but I don't know what happened on that trip. Over the years I would get bits and pieces, but I'm so thankful I was never there. There were girls in complete denial, the ones that refused to admit that it happened, and refused to testify. The Olympics was on the line, and then she was gone, never to coach in Canada again. She disappeared. Our once strong, solid group of girls evaporated. Some switched clubs, some retired. One girl, the girl, followed her out of the country. A few of us stayed, found our footing and started again; and our assistant coach stepped in and brought us back to life.

She was so different: calm and patient. I would go to her when I was having an awful day, and work with her because I knew she could help me recover from my frustration and turn my practice around. She gained my trust and respect from the very beginning, and I wasn't always the easiest gymnast to work with. I was stubborn and moody, way too hard on myself, and would let my head get the best of me. As I got older I noticed this more and more, and knew the type of pressure that was on me.

As a younger gymnast, I knew I was talented and confident. I would walk out there and do my thing without a care in the world. As I moved up to the next national level from novice to junior, I felt the heat, and with a new coach and a scandal behind us, it was hard to move on. The community was so small that everyone knew everything about everyone, and the gossip was horrible. Rivalries between gymnasts, clubs and coaches were rampant, and it's never changed. It can be a war zone, and you can feel so judged and trapped all in the same second. I was scared that we were being tested with a new coach and a new look. What if this big change that shook all our worlds had left us struggling to pick up the pieces? But we had worked so well together to prepare for the new season, and it showed. The next year she had the novice, junior and senior national champions, and became the most successful coach in Canada. I think this is when it all changed.

At the time I was in junior high, and my teammate and best friend, Sarah, who was in high school, would come and pick me up after school every day and drive me to the gym. We trained six days a week like usual, and everything seemed to be flawless until that little thing called pressure started to close the gym walls all around us, draining us and suffocating the spirit that once was there.

Sarah was like an older sister that I looked up to, and we had trained together for years. She couldn't be more opposite than me: tall, thin and blonde. I was a little, short muscular thing, dark skin and dark hair. She was the pretty one. As we got older, she always had a boyfriend or a trail of boys behind her, and I was so envious. Everything seemed so easy for her.

We travelled the world together with late nights in small, cold hotel rooms, sharing a tiny bed somewhere thousands of miles away from home, eating candy and watching TV, jumping on our beds, and laughing all night. I loved and idolized her. We were silly and stupid, but I learned so much from her: how to work in the gym, be a girl outside sport, do my makeup and hair. I spent more time with her than my family. She was my family. No matter what happened, we would always be together, and some days I would look at the two of us in the mirror as we were warming up in the gym, and I wanted it to stay this way forever. We were like yin and yang, sharing all our secrets and our lives. In the gym, she pushed me to be better. We were different gymnasts completely, which was probably a good thing—different styles, body types and abilities. That's what made us so special. But we learned from each other and pushed each other with each of our successes. I wish things had stayed that easy.

Sarah was two years older than me, and we had never competed against each other. When she was senior national champion, I was junior champion. But there was nowhere else for her to go after that, and so I would turn fifteen and become senior, and for the first time we would be going head to head. Up until that point my career from the outside had been pretty perfect: novice national champion, two-time junior national champion, and junior pan American champion—beating the Americans and Venezuelans in Caracas to take the title. That was the first time I put my name on the map, and I was officially on the international radar as a girl to watch. The Pan American championships brought together the best gymnasts from all of the Americas, and I knew that this was my chance to take it all, to take a step towards my future in the sport as a champion, as the next big thing. We flew down to Caracas. I was only thirteen, and my mom came down with us along with other parents. We stayed on a military base in Venezuela. There were men with machine guns everywhere, the heat was a killer, and the Spanish was fast and incomprehensible. I was overwhelmed. We would sleep with soaking wet, freezing cold towels just to get through the nights in the heat, and wake up all the time to girls screaming that there were lizards and bugs in their beds. I'll never forget it. That heat was unlike anything I had ever experienced, and we were exhausted. I remember asking myself what we were doing there, as trying to get acclimatized in the gym took us days. We would watch the Venezuelan team not even break a sweat as we were dying on the side, panting, guzzling water as if we had been lost in a desert for days. It felt like there was a rock on my chest and I couldn't breathe. What a mess, all eyes were on me as I tried to train. Every coach and every judge from all the different countries would come out of the woodwork and skulk around the competition floor, sit in the stands or at the judges' table. They would sit there, watch and gossip to their friends and teams. God knows what they were saying. I never wanted to know, but when we used to watch our competitors, there was nothing good being said. It was either silence, or the criticism would flow from your lips so easily it was second nature. You were constantly comparing yourself to others and to your teammates. Vicious. Brutal. Competitive. Like any sport, if you're representing your country, you're there to win. I knew it, we all knew it; and I could feel my knees shake as I stood there waiting to compete that first day of competition. I was barely a teenager and carried the weight of my team on my shoulders. It was up to me to lead the way, to do this for us.

When I came back with the title of Champion, I was on fire. I won a big international competition that year in Portugal, walking off the plane with five gold trophies to my family's hysteria in the airport. My gold was heavier than I was, and bigger than me, and I went back to junior high with all these adventure stories from exotic places. The food, the people, the hotels. I began to live in the airport. After my first trip to France when I was eleven, it just never stopped. I had to be out on the world circuit, going to all the major competitions, letting the judges see my face. I had to make a name for myself. Canadians are nobody in this sport until they prove it. It's harsh, but true. Eastern Europeans dominate the rhythmic gymnastics scene, and they always have. There have been a few North Americans to squeeze in there, some dark horses that have popped out of nowhere to shock and awe, to throw a wrench into the well oiled machine. But it takes years and years to build that kind of reputation, that kind of name that pushes the judges to help you out a bit, and push you into that next range of scores. If you constantly proved to them that you were consistent, talented, passionate and hungry for it, they would reward you.

So many people over the years would ask me how I could be a part of such a subjective sport, a sport where the best person doesn't always win, and having to face all the unfairness, injustice and hard feelings. But I never saw it like that. I could never control the judges. What they did was out of my hands. But I could control myself, and I could make it impossible for them to not notice me and look at me like I was world-class. I could make them give me the scores if I didn't allow any room for error, any room for them to doubt that I deserved to be among the best in the world. And that's what got me through all the years, all the struggles. It was that quest for perfection, that mountain to climb, to find my potential and make others realize it, to make judges, to make the world, see my strength and my skills. Looking back on it now, I never realized how many years it would take and what I would have to go through before I finally got to that point where I was one of them, in the top ten in the world, comfortably training next to the world champion, and watching her like I could take her on. I was thirteen when I was junior pan American champion, just a baby beginning her career. I had no idea what was in store for me, but I think my coach did all along.

My coach and I always had an interesting relationship right from the start. Never best friends, never working harmoniously together, but we had an understanding, some secret bond that neither one of us knew about. I respected her and knew that I had to trust her and she had to trust me if it was going to work, or else it would all fall apart. There were many times where I doubted this trust, doubted whether she even cared about me at all. But there were times when I have never been happier in my life, and she was there standing behind me. There were moments when my body took over and everything clicked, and I was doing the impossible, feeling something I had never felt before, creating an energy that would make people stop and stare. She brought that out in me. There were times when she would put her hand on my back or shoot me a smile like, "Wow, that's it!" And I have never been happier. We had done something, created something so beautiful, but we never got along as a coach and athlete usually would. We are both very strong people, very set in our ways. I never thought we were similar before, but maybe, just maybe, we were. We both wanted to win, that's for sure. We wanted success. There's nothing wrong with saying that. I was proud to say that I was going for gold. It fuelled me, and if you want to get to the Olympics, you have to be able to say it, speak the words out loud, set milestones for yourself, and believe in them. Don't doubt it for a second. I know she knew how badly I wanted to become an Olympian, but with my first year of senior approaching, she had two of us to deal with: My teammate, the seasoned champion; and the new wildcard, me, the unpredictable one. That transition wasn't easy, it was horrible. Training became more difficult, I couldn't do anything right, and I would never make it as a senior if I was going to look the way I was looking. I don't know if she was scared that if I didn't do well it would mean she failed as a coach, but the tension between us grew. I couldn't work with her anymore. One bad day turned into a week, turned into a month. She would scream until her face was red, so frustrated with me and my attitude. I was my own worst enemy then, at an age where I had had enough of people telling me that I was wrong all the time, and that I wasn't good enough. I would stare at her with these eyes, screaming at her silently in my head, all of it coming through my glance. She would hate it when I looked at her like that, and would call my mother every day to the point where my mom would dread picking up the phone and seeing her number. "What has Alex done this time?" I would storm out of the gym to get air, wanting to put my fist through a wall, trying so hard to not let her see me cry. But there were days when that's all I could do. "Why couldn't I be more like Sarah?" she used to say. I loathed that sentence for so long; even now I cringe at it. I wasn't Sarah. I was just Alex. I wasn't easy, I wasn't perfect. If she could have understood that when I got frustrated it wasn't me rebelling against her, I was the hardest critic on myself, and I would shut down inside, so angry that I couldn't do it. So angry at what she thought or who she thought I was. The things that were said in the gym those years are hard for me to even recount as I've tried to block them all from my mind. In one ear, out the other, they say. You would never want those words, those stinging words, to stick with you for too long. They would bring unstoppable tears to your eyes, heaviness to your limbs, and an emptiness inside.

After endless days of the same thing, the same unproductive trainings, the "talks" with my parents... I began to do it, get so angry, to spite them, to spite all of them. This included those who would come to the gym to see how I was training, the judges that could never remember my name and only Sarah's, and the coaches that would pick at my every move. I wish I was one of those people that could hide their emotions, but mine went right to my face. I couldn't help it. I was an open book. What you see is definitely what you get, and when I am unhappy, believe me, you know it. My stubborn attitude killed me, and I wanted so desperately to shake it off and show my coach, show everyone, that I had this talent and that I wasn't just wasting time in the gym; that I wasn't just giving my coach a hard time. It was easier to be upset and angry than to be perfectly happy and not good enough. This way I had an excuse. After all these years I finally get it. I didn't want to give her the satisfaction of thinking that she had hurt me. So instead of getting sad, I would get angry. So mad, in fact, that I could rebound and break through this invisible barrier I had placed in front of myself. Either that or it would take me to some of the darkest places I have ever been. She had a little black book that I hated. I could feel her eyes on me even when I wasn't looking, recording my every move, and I always wondered what she wrote in there. I would keep her up at night, she used to say. With weeks to go before a competition, she sometimes threatened to not let me compete, and was always questioning what was wrong with me, over and over. There was nothing wrong with me, it was just so difficult to stay positive when all I wanted to do was curl up in a ball and hide away. There was a year when she would make me come in on my day off and work only one apparatus because I wasn't strong enough in it. She would sit there with her little black book, and I would go over every single element until I could do ten perfectly. I would sulk as I walked into the gym, and it tore my mom up to see me this way. She didn't know if this was the right thing for me. I didn't even know at the time. But my coach made me do it for my own good. The repetition was mind numbing. Being alone with her, so quiet you could hear a pin drop, I ran skill after skill until my legs couldn't take anymore. She would talk to me and I couldn't even look at her, my eyes always on the floor. I was scared that I wouldn't be able to hold in what I wanted to tell her if I was looking at her face. If I stared into her eyes, I was terrified that all the frustration, all the anger I had would come flying out of my mouth. On occasion it did. I wasn't perfect and will never be, and when I hit my breaking points I had to leave the gym or say something.

Regardless of what she thought, I always knew when I was working and when I wasn't. I would give up sometimes as there was some place inside of me that checked all my goals at the door and just wanted to be the sullen teenager that I never got to be. The normal kid that never got to rebel, never got to lead a normal life. All I knew was that my coach was one of the best coaches in the world, taking athletes to every Olympics for decades, and having more champions and training more girls all over the world than anyone I had ever worked with. I got to the Olympics because of her. I wasn't in it alone, and looking back on my career I know why she did what she had to do. I understand that she had to push me as hard as she did, that she had to make me angry to take me to that next level; and I realize that she had a plan all along after all. She supported me, my country supported me, and I felt like every coach, parent, judge and athlete wanted this for me too, which is pretty rare to say in a sport as competitive as mine. It wouldn't be easy, but I think she always knew that I had it in me to go to the Olympics. Back when it was just Sarah and I, and I was the new kid on the block, she imagined having both of us become Olympians together.

Canada as a team would have to place in the top ten to get two spots at the Olympics—the fairytale ending. But we were getting ahead of ourselves because I hadn't even competed as a senior yet, and who knew how I would make the transition, the big leap into the big leagues. I was hoping to be top six in Canada, and just to make the national team would have been more than enough. But over the off season, I grew into a young woman. I shot up, and was all of a sudden all legs. I had a more sophisticated style, more emotional connection with the audience. I was coming into my own, and it worked for me. Our first national meet, Sarah and I were seeded one and two: on top of the world. My coach couldn't have been happier. That was the first and last time I ever felt like I had nothing to lose. I was there as a newbie, the young one, and there were no real expectations, no real pressure. It was unbelievable, and I had my best performance ever. I was so overwhelmed as I stood on the podium next to Sarah, ahead of all the girls I had looked up to. It was a surreal moment the instant I realized I really did have a shot at the Olympics. I was a contender now. All my attention turned to Sarah. She was my competition. I loved her so much, but every time I would compete it would be to inch closer and closer to her, and eventually surpass her. I don't think any other athlete would have a different mindset. We were best friends, but when you're out there, you're out there to win, and that's not a question. It must have been difficult for our coach to see the internal battle between us. Internationally, there is always one gymnast from every country that is seen as the champion, seen as number one over the rest. For the Eastern Europeans, their top two usually have this special status, this invisible halo over them, signalling their separation from the rest, above the pack. It didn't work that way for North and South Americans. We put all our eggs in one basket, and every country threw all their support behind one girl, their champion. In a judged sport like rhythmic gymnastics, there are only so many girls that can squeeze into the top twenty. That was the fight. The never-ending fight. Realistically, even if I was just as good as Sarah, there was only room for one of us. But that never stopped me from trying. I was a fighter, and I would continue to travel the world and train until I believed I couldn't go further than I had.

It was two years out to the Olympics and we were in travelling mode. Still trying to manage high school at the same time, I would photocopy hundreds and hundreds of pages of textbooks to take with me around the world. Our suitcases were filled with training gear, books, homework, music and equipment. It would take a full two days to get ready for one of those six-week adventures. All our competitions were in Europe and Asia, so we would group them together, and on one trip, try and hit a few competitions. If they were a week or two apart we would set up camp in some country to train with their national team. We were nomads roaming around the world, living in airports, and sitting on plane after plane. It all became routine. New city, new bed. But it had a familiar feel to it. The people on the world cup circuit are the same. You began to see the same coaches and gymnasts. We made friends with people that I still have in my life now. You learn bits and pieces of languages and customs; sightsee and travel through the city differently to how a tourist would. We would billet with families sometimes, and spend a week living with a German or French family, experimenting with the public transportation system, lugging all our equipment and gym bags on and off transit. Most of the time we were wearing leg warmers and black tights that made us stand out even more. We didn't care, we were there to train. That was our job, and it was who we were. The midnight snack runs and little moments we got to escape, such as coming back from a competition at 2 a.m. in Tokyo and running around the streets like it was daytime, are my favourite memories. Sometimes we were rewarded with a day off, and hit the beach, which was always so close yet so far away from where we trained. Copacabana in Brazil. The white sands in the south of Spain or Portugal. The hot rocks in a little town in Greece. The north shores of France. My life was something out of a movie, but I never noticed it then. There were nights when we couldn't sleep and we would stay up watching DVDs from back home that our parents sent away with us. We could watch an entire season of a TV show in a few days. We would be so exhausted from the day of training—always an early morning and sometimes training twice a day or competing—the last thing we wanted to do was go outside and explore. Once we had all showered and eaten, we slid into our sweats and made our room (wherever it was) our home. Nothing felt better than jumping into bed and just "being". We would let our muscles relax by lying on our backs with our legs on the walls, reading or listening to music. I tried to keep a journal over the years, but it was so hard to describe the emotions you felt some days. You would never want to write them down, or couldn't. Things you couldn't admit or didn't want to think about. Homesickness wasn't an option. I would avoid calling my family because hearing their voices was enough to feel it in the back of my throat. As we travelled more and more, it became easier to call home because it felt like Europe was our home. We were used to it, used to the culture, the food, the languages and the people. I knew what to expect and what we were supposed to do while we were there. Train and train well. Compete and compete well. That was it. Seemed simple enough, right?

We would pick up and leave our lives, our friends, our relationships, and our family behind. Everything was scheduled around my trips. My good friends always tried to make me feel included, and still asked me to come out even though they knew I couldn't. They would still invite me to their cottages or plan as if I would be able to come to their birthdays or the opening night of their play. They wouldn't hold it against me when I had to cancel. I'm not going to say I never saw them because I did, and I did everything in my power to make it when I said I would, to be there for them like they were there for me. But it was difficult to be my friend, and I lost so many of them along the way. The invites stopped coming, the phone calls weren't there. When I was so far away I had my teammates to rely on, and they became my sisters. Whether we got along all the time or not, we were closer than we ever thought.

Chapter 2:
In The Shadows

The years leading up to the 2004 Olympics are a blur now. They seem like a lifetime ago because I was a different person then. My whole life, I always thought that these were my Games, my one shot at becoming an Olympian. I planned on retiring while still in high school, and getting out of Toronto for university. I thought I had it all figured out. I would write it down in my journal and plan out exactly what I would do with all my free time once I was done.

Athens became the only focus. Even though it may have seemed like a long shot to some, it wasn't to me. Everything was going according to plan so far, why would it ever change? I couldn't have been more wrong. Just when you think everything's alright, when you think you can predict the ending of the story, life throws you a curveball—hard and fast.

I had been competing for nine years at this point, and all my trips, the flights, the hotels, food, and training were covered by my family. My parents literally funded my career, and would help Sarah and her family as much as they could. I don't think I realized how selfless you have to be, how much love you have to have for a person to do that. I will never be able to repay them. One year before Olympic Qualifiers, the U.S. team approached my coach at a competition. I'll never forget this. I remember thinking it odd that Sarah and I were in this room with all these people, and I had no idea what they were about to say. They had found out that both of us were dual citizens, both able to compete for the U.S.

at any given time, if we chose to. They offered us the world to compete for the States, giving us a better chance to qualify for the Olympics.

I didn't know it then, but the Canadian Olympic Committee placed strict standards on all Canadian athletes attempting to qualify for the Olympics, standards which ironically were harder than most international requirements. Every Canadian athlete had to be in the top twelve in the world in their sport to go to Athens. I was kept in the dark completely. At this time in my career, that result was impossible. There was no way I would have ever made it even if I had put in the competition of a lifetime. I wasn't there yet, and wasn't at that kind of level. So there we were, our coach completely supportive of this idea, telling us to think about it: "Don't make a decision now, but all expenses would be covered". Money wouldn't be an issue anymore. I remember thinking what a great idea it was. My Olympic dream could actually come true. But when I got home, reality hit me. I sat in my kitchen with my parents, and there was an ache in my stomach as we talked about it. Around and around the table we went, weighing out all the options and outcomes. But in the end, it was making me sick to my stomach. I could never wear another flag on my back, sing another anthem. I am proud of my American heritage and value it greatly. My father fought for his country, and my grandparents took a chance and left it all behind in Italy to go to America to give their children a better life. I love where my family is from, and I understand the strong tie they have to the U.S. It's their home. But I was born and raised in Toronto, and my community was there. I was a four-time national champion at the time. I had won medals for Canada and had carried a rivalry with the U.S. team most of my life. I just couldn't imagine leaving. I couldn't do it. It didn't feel right to me.

My parents knew that the possibility of me making the Olympics under the Canadian standard was incredibly slim, but they let me make my decision on my own. They were so proud of me for taking a stance and not backing down. A part of me wishes

I could have done it just so the financial burden on my family could have stopped. I told them over and over again, "If you want me to do it, I'll do it"; and for them I would have. They sacrificed so much for me, it would be the least that I could do. But they never thought I was a burden, they never complained. They just did what they could. So it was settled, I was definitely not going. I would stay and take my chances representing Canada. But Sarah decided to make the switch. I didn't quite know what to say. It would all be so different now. The U.S. had taken our national champion, but she would still train with me and our coach in Canada. This is when it all got confusing. This is when someone should have stepped in and done what was best for the both of us. But no one did.

Our coach needed to choose who she was going to coach, but she didn't. She couldn't. She coached both of us, and at the start of the season she could say she had both the U.S. and Canadian senior national champions under her wing. At first it felt like everything was the same, but when we started competing it couldn't have been more different. Everyone was so confused about why Sarah was all of a sudden "American," and why their Canadian national champion had been replaced. They announced her as Canadian a few times, and the two of us were always together because of our coach, so people assumed she was still number one and I was number two. This affected me more than I let anyone know. My coach was now with Canada and America, a team that we were constantly trying to beat over the years. There are hundreds of gymnasts that show up at world championships, and a well-known coach always has *one* star. There is always a one and a two, and we all knew it. Even as national champion that first year, I was still stuck in the shadows. It felt like I had lost my teammate. We were the perfect team, but I wanted her to be happy, and if this is what she wanted to do then I would respect her decision. At age fifteen and seventeen, we were acting like grown-ups. The whole experience taught me that I needed to grow up quickly, and it was an experience that propelled me into a leadership role, as all of a sudden I was team captain. As a young champion, I was now the one to set an example, and owed it to myself to figure out what it was going to be, what kind of person I really was. I had eight months to get my footing as national champion before walking into my first world championships, my first Olympic Qualifiers, and my only shot at Athens.

That year flew by so fast. Before I knew it I was in Bulgaria at a six-week training camp, and then Budapest, Hungary for Worlds. That camp was one of the hardest, most gruelling camps I had ever been to. We lived in the gym, a few floors up above the ballet studios, and we hardly left. There was no reason to. Five of us crammed onto three beds and a mattress on the floor. Sarah and I took the floor to avoid the temper tantrums from the rest of them. It was dark and damp, with one bathroom and minimal hot water. The TV screened nothing but European MTV, on constantly, and there was a fridge with water, fruit and yogurt. When we could, we would head out to the bazaar, the local market that was behind the gym, and bring back cereal to munch on during those nights we couldn't sleep or in between practices when we couldn't find the energy to go to the cafeteria. There was a restaurant joined to the training complex where we would have preset meals determined by our coaches. I was starving half the time, constantly searching for food. It was the only thing that took my mind off the pain in my back or the pulsing ache in my lifeless legs. We would bring back food to the room even though it brought all kinds of bugs into our temporary home. We didn't care. It was worth it to have that piece of bread, that little piece of heaven.

Every morning when our alarm clock would go off, no one would stir. It would turn off, and we would all lay there, awake, in silence, summoning energy to battle the day. We would dance around each other getting ready, eyes half closed, iPods in. One by one we would head downstairs to the ballet room. After a gruelling two hours of ballet, we would start our real practice. The gym had a huge ceiling, three competition carpets next to each other packed full of girls, music blaring from all angles, coaches yelling, and the familiar sound of apparatus hitting the floor or someone's body. I would sit in splits, resting, head down on the floor, waiting for the coaches to arrive knowing this would be the last time I could relax for the next four hours. They would come in, coffee in one hand, wearing stilettos and sunglasses, all dressed up for us, I used to think. They would laugh and talk fast in Bulgarian, and we could only imagine what they were saying. And then it would all begin. We trained for four minute-and-a-half events, two in the morning and two in the afternoon, over and over, with numbing repetition. I would have to perform each event twice, perfectly, plus some half parts before switching apparatus, and this could take an hour or two or three depending on the day. It could take all day if you were off your game, repeating your routine over until you couldn't feel your legs. We're only human after all. There were only a few of us training at the same time, unlike at home when you had to fight to share the carpet and the attention of your coach. Here, all eyes were on you all the time. After any long trip away from home my endurance was always shot, the first thing to go. That first day overseas at the gym, my legs were always Jell-O. I could barely finish an event without the lactic acid attacking my legs, turning them into stone. That feeling made my stomach turn. But that was no excuse, and I had to work through it no matter how much it hurt. We would have a two-hour lunch break, and would eat immediately and go back to the room and collapse into a deep sleep. Still wearing sweat-soaked tights, we would pull on our leg warmers and sweatshirts and hide among the covers. I would fall into a coma the minute I hit the hard pillow. When the alarm went off for the second time that day, groans came around the room. Now muscles were not just sore, but tired too. We were freezing after keeping those once warm clothes hugged to our bodies, and with makeup smeared all over our faces, hair out of whack, we gave ourselves five minutes to wash our faces, pull ourselves together, and then a little slower this time, head downstairs for the next four hours of training.

Warming up for the second time was the most painful. Your

body shuts down and doesn't want to stretch. You somehow find it in yourself to sink a little deeper as one foot hooks onto the back of the chair, and you slide your other leg out behind you. You could feel your muscles lengthening as you breathed through the pain, sinking a bit deeper. Overspilts was something that seemed so natural to us yet was so disturbing to others, and even my sister could never get used to seeing me contort my body in this way. The second time around took so much more energy to train with expression, and I had to force myself to keep my eyes off the floor and engage the imaginary audience as I performed to the music. I still don't know how we got through it. The windows in the gym became blackened with nightfall, and the lights were harsher without the sunlight. We would collapse on the floor to start conditioning, praying that it would be over soon. I would repeat it over in my head that I was almost done, whispering to myself as I used the last bit of energy I had to keep moving. By the time we got to the room, we were walking zombies. I hardly had any energy to write in my journal, and all I could do was eat a little, read or watch TV as my eyes glazed over. When we turned out the lights, my favourite part of the day was lying there awake in the pitch dark. I would listen to the rise and fall of my teammates' chests as they fell into a deep sleep. I could hear the wind outside, and had the moonlight on my face. I could live in that moment for a lifetime. It was the satisfaction of knowing what you accomplished that day; that you pushed your body through it, and now you could feel every muscle relaxing, sinking down into the mattress. Nothing ever felt so good, but it only lasted a few moments before I couldn't fight it any longer and fell victim to my dreams.

I would cross off the days in my journal as we got closer to Worlds. I would either be flying home with everything I had ever wanted tightly in my grasp, or I didn't even want to think about the other option. It hadn't even occurred to me that I would be coming home with bad news. It was all about the task in front of me in that moment. There was no future, no past. It didn't matter what I did the day before, the week before. I was standing in Budapest ready to do what no one expected—come in as the underdog and blow everyone away. That week was the most important week of my life; and in my head there was nothing after it. The days slowed and the week seemed stretched as we settled into the hotel, the new city, and the new vibe. You could feel the tension everywhere: in the hallways, the dining room, the gym. It was cutthroat. Everyone was thinking the same thing. This was our moment. This was it.

Worlds was held in a huge arena the size of two football fields. The gym was the biggest thing I had ever seen in my life, and I was completely intimidated. One half of the arena had twelve competition carpets divided with big, thick black curtains that ran from the 40-foot ceiling down to the floor. It was a maze that I was continuously lost in for the entire week. Every floor had a number, and you rotated between carpets allowing each country to have training time. The competition arena had two competition carpets and two, three-tiered judging panels divided by a mesh curtain. So when you were out there, there was a girl competing right beside you at the exact same time. When I saw that, I remember starting to freak out with that nervous energy bubbling up inside of me. No one had ever competed like that before on our team. Team Canada was so young that year, such babies, and we had no idea what we were walking into. I trained like I had never done gymnastics before, completely terrified, shaking on the inside and doubting every step. It was as if my feet were unsure of the floor beneath them, and my head was up in the clouds somewhere. It was brutal. I didn't understand what my body was doing. It was as if it was disconnected from my head and I couldn't mesh the two together again. My coach was running back and forth between the Team Canada practices and the American team to coach Sarah, because it was her who really had the shot at the Olympics. All our coach had to do with the U.S. team was rank in the top twenty: a very realistic goal for her. I knew I wasn't her main focus, and I knew that even though I wasn't training as well as I should have been, she had Sarah, and that made her happy. I was still number two, but I was number one in my head. As Canadian Senior National Champion, I was going to fight to the end. I would be unforgettable. At least I would make my coach remember that.

A few days before it all started, my parents flew over the Atlantic to support me. I remember seeing them down the street for the first time in front of my hotel as I walked back from the gym one day. I dropped my bag and ran so fast to them, and had never been happier to see them in my life. My mom was crying as usual, and she could see I had changed, had grown up, that I had a focus to me that wasn't there before I left. With them there, my nerves subsided. My family came to stand there beside me as I walked out into that stadium in front of all the judges and all the people. But it was as if I was performing only for them. I could feel them in the stands; hear my dad cheering for me. His voice, so loud and low, boomed across the arena down to the floor. They wanted this for me so badly. They also knew the pieces that they would have to pick up and put back together if I didn't make it. I can't imagine being a parent and watching your child go out there and put it all out on the line, and fail. That must be one of the hardest things to see because you can't do anything, you have no control. My parents had to stand there and know how scared I was. They had to feel my heart beat when they pulled me in for that last hug before I competed. They knew what was on the line, and couldn't do a thing about it. But my family was and always is so positive, and they had never-ending hope that I had it in me to do this. I knew it too.

I put in four great routines those first two days of competition, and I remember thinking, "Wow, maybe I had really done it!" There are about 120 gymnasts that compete at world championships. The best three or four from every country compete for their world ranking, which is something that would define the type of gymnast you were and the level you belonged in. It set you up for the next season, and could make or break you. As if that wasn't enough pressure, to qualify for the Olympics you have to rank in the top twenty. Everyone gets a country spot and a buy in to the Games. There are four wild cards picked to help ensure equal representation between all continents. Because rhythmic gymnastics is so dominated by Europe, Oceania always gets a spot, Africa usually gets one or two, and then North America, South America or Asia, depending on who qualifies automatically. If a North or South American qualifies in the top twenty, there's no wild card for these continents. And so with Sarah in the top twenty, my wild card option went out the window. But I didn't want a wild card. I wanted to qualify outright. The wild cards are always a sensitive subject across the board in all sports. There is no real standard for those cards, and that could mean a gymnast who is ranked sixtieth or higher in the world could get a spot over someone who is in the top twenty-five. So for me, I didn't want to hear it, there was no wild card talk. There was only the top twenty. That was all I had in my head, but that year I was consistently ranked between twentieth and thirtieth place at world cups. Close, but not quite there.

On any given day, it was anyone's shot to squeeze in. Because of the sheer amount of competitors that year, the competition was divided into four groups that competed all day. I finished my last routine in the morning of the second day, and then it was a waiting game. Your name would be up on the scoreboard, and you would watch it get knocked down one by one as countries were finishing up. It was almost all over, and I sat there with my parents thinking that it was going to happen. I had received higher marks than I had gotten all year, and I was sitting around eighteenth position nearing the end. I could barely look, and was getting sick to my stomach waiting for scores to pop up there. My coach was sitting in the stands with me, calculating if I had come in the top twelve in any single event to make a case against the Canadian Olympic Committee standard back home in Canada. Even if I had come in the top twenty, there was a really good possibility that Canada wouldn't send me to the Olympics because I wasn't in the top twelve. Before we even had the news, my heart was slowly cracking, my breathing slowed, and things around me got fuzzy.

I sat linking arms with my mom, hanging onto her tightly like I was a child, not believing that we were sitting there knowing that it was all over.

My parents were so supportive, and are still so supportive of everything I do. They are so hopeful, so loving and positive, and truly believed we could fight this. But I knew better. As it ended up, this wasn't my fairytale ending. This wasn't the classic underdog rising to the top against all odds story. This was real life. A gymnast whom I had beaten all year, and who had received three similar, lower marks, scored an out-of-nowhere high fourth score to everyone's surprise, and slipped into twentieth spot by 0.1. I was twenty-first. My name came up, and we all just sat there not knowing what to do. My teammates hung their heads. Everyone was saying they were sorry, but I couldn't hear it. My coach was distraught as her dream of having two Olympians at the same time was crushed. Sarah had easily qualified, and I could see that everyone was torn between being happy for her and sad for me. Even though she was with the American team, she was Canadian through and through. She had grown up with us, she had lived with my family, and we had paid for her trips and supported her when her family couldn't. Our community in Canada was behind her every step of the way, so it was as if a Canadian had qualified. But I couldn't be happy for her because I was devastated. My whole world came crashing down all around me in an instant. So quickly it all fell apart. I don't remember much of that day, but I somehow made it back to the hotel by myself. I didn't want to be with my parents or my teammates, I wanted to be alone. I put in my earphones and took my Discman out to the balcony. The sun was setting and it was a beautiful night in Hungary. I stood there like a statue leaning on the railing, looking out at the horizon, not really looking at anything in particular, and not being able to focus on anything. The sun was dying, and so was I. Tears streamed down my face, and I didn't wipe them away. I let them stay there, staining my face, stuck in the memory. I didn't want to wipe them away and forget what had happened. I was going to torture myself. I wasn't hysterical,

I could breathe. I wasn't heaving sobs or making a scene. I was silent, which scared everyone. My teammate and one of my best friends, Yana from Montreal, came back from the gym quietly. She slipped into the room unnoticed and came out on the balcony, and without a word put her arm around me and stood there with me looking out into the sunset. I never told her what that meant to me to have her there, what it meant to have someone be there with me as I broke down inside. I put my head on her shoulder and closed my eyes. Her heart broke for me. Yana is one of those unbelievable people with an incredibly good heart, beautiful inside and out. She was such a hard worker and so passionate that I could watch her on the carpet for hours. She was a role model for us all, and I will never forget what she did for me.

It was so quiet. I stood there for a long time, not being able to move. I had let everyone down: my country, my coach, my team, all the girls back home who were rooting for me, my family, my friends, my school, my community. I was a failure. A loser coming home empty handed, not good enough. I couldn't stop thinking about what a disappointment I was. This was not just something I could be upset about, shake off and continue on with my life. This was a deal breaker. My coach came to my room and was giving me tough love, reminding me that I had to compete tomorrow for the all around competition. Only the top thirty compete again, and this will determine my world ranking heading into the next year. How could she think about the future? There was no future for me. I didn't talk to Sarah that night. I couldn't bring myself to do it. She left me alone because I'm sure she didn't know what to say. We both were speechless, it was horrible. Two best friends, like sisters, who shared everything, who loved each other more than anything, stuck in a situation that neither one of us was strong enough to deal with. We were so close, and had imagined living next door to each other when we were all grown up with our kids being best friends. She was everything to me, but we would never be the same again, as much as it pains me to say that. That one day changed everything.

The next day, every time I closed my eyes, all I saw was that scoreboard. Competing was the last thing I wanted to do, and I didn't want to be anywhere near a gym. When I walked into the training area, the sadness washed away and I was angry. Having Sarah there made me feel at home, made me feel like we were back in Toronto getting ready for another competition like old times. It gave me a sense of reassurance that everything would be okay. I don't know how or why, but I found this fire that drove me through that day. With nothing to lose, I ate the carpet up out there. If I wasn't good enough, then I would show them just what I was capable of. Event after event, I nailed it, putting a smile on my coach's face that I hadn't seen in a long time. We had done something that day that neither of us thought I was capable of doing. When all was said and done, I was ranked sixteenth in the world—Olympic worthy, Olympic level. I wasn't sure whether to laugh or cry, and my family, my supporters, and my team were ecstatic. They were crying over what I had accomplished, and everyone was so overwhelmed. They knew I had just shown how I deserved to be at the Olympics. How I had proved it. I was supposed to be there, and it gave me the confidence to walk around with my head held high. I wasn't a failure, I was sixteenth in the world in my first year competing at this level, which was something that could take a gymnast years of competing to achieve. But it was so bittersweet. Every time I would let myself be proud, a flash of disappointment would take over. It still wasn't good enough, it was the wrong day. I needed it two days ago. I couldn't understand why life was so unfair, why this had happened to me. This wasn't supposed to happen, how could it all be ending this way?

When I got home, I had a lot to think about. I was unbearable to be around, so angry, and I hated everything and everyone. I was miserable. I felt lost for the first time in my life, and could barely recognize myself. It was one of the darkest times of my life, and I couldn't shake the feeling of inadequacy, of failure. I was embarrassed to go to school, to go to training, to see anyone. I couldn't face the constant reminder that I wasn't good enough.

I never thought I would have to make the decision that would affect not only my life, but also my family too. I always thought I would retire after the 2004 Olympics, and that would be it. But now that I hadn't qualified, I was seriously considering stepping away from it for good. I didn't want any part of the sport, and I never thought I would compete again. It was all over. I remember my coach coming over to my house and sitting at the kitchen table with a cup of coffee, talking to my mother and I, explaining that there was still a shot for me, that we could fight for a ranking wild card because I was twenty-first. There's usually one card that either goes to the next girl in line or to a girl from a developing country, but they have to meet certain requirements. "The card went to Cape Verde, but we could fight it," they promised me. She had placed near the one hundredth spot at Worlds, which is nowhere near the standard, and there may be a shot we could win it. I remember throwing all logic out the window and clinging to hope, to that one shred of chance that this could work. Deep down I never wanted to quit, I loved the sport too much; but I needed a reason to keep going. I needed something to work towards or else I would be lost, and was so stubborn I didn't want to keep training for the love of the sport—I wanted the results, I wanted the achievements. I wanted the Olympics. So I stuck it out and kept telling myself that I would get this wild card and then we would go up against the Olympic Committee with their top twelve standard. It would mean a battle, but it could happen. It had to happen.

We were all living in a dream world, and I really thought it would all work out. That year, I competed well, but my heart wasn't there. Something was missing. As Athens came closer, I had to face the harsh reality that it wasn't going to happen. We all did. And it was worse than anything I had felt in Budapest. I couldn't even go to Sarah's congratulations party, her send off before the Games. I remember making that decision and feeling awful about it, but I had to do it for me. I wished her the best and was so happy for her, but it would have been a constant reminder of what I had lost. I wouldn't ruin her day, her big moment. My presence there would have just reminded her that she was realizing her dream and I wasn't. Either way, it was a lose–lose situation. No one else saw it like that, and my coach and the rhythmic community were so upset I wasn't there, and I heard about it for months afterwards, but I didn't care. I did what I thought was right for the both of us. It wasn't fair to have me put a damper on it, and it wasn't right to make her feel like she couldn't celebrate in front of me, which I know she would have because that was Sarah, and I love her for that. Athens was her Games, her time, and I watched her compete from my couch, so proud of her. She was a part of my family, and we were all behind her. I was so nervous for her and wanted only the best, but I knew that when she retired it was never going to be the same. It would be an end of an era. The end of Sarah and Alex.

Watching the Olympics come and go made me want to hate my sport, hate everything. I was a 16-year-old sullen teenager, and I was miserable and thought my life was over. I stopped training for the first time in a long time, and I just couldn't get out of my funk. I wanted to cry and scream, and I did, giving my family hell when all they were trying to do was understand what I was going through, and be there for me. But I didn't let them. I started Grade 12 and had to face everyone at school asking me if I went to the Olympics, telling me they watched for me but didn't see me. "Did you end up going?" My head was spinning. Everywhere I turned it was still Olympics madness, and it had enveloped my life. I was back in the gym with my coach for the first time without Sarah, and I was trying to get used to the change, to this new life. But I couldn't. I didn't know what I was working towards; I didn't have a goal, and was thinking about retiring again. I was so confused. My sister came to my room one night, I had been crying for no reason again, and she asked me, "What makes you happy?" I looked at her, and in that moment knew how lucky I was to have people in my life that cared about me. I needed to lean on them, and to let them help me through this. She told me that the Olympics was just one competition, and it didn't take away the years of memories my sport had given me: the adventures, the experiences. That it couldn't take away how it made me feel when I was out there. And she was right. For once, I realized that I hadn't been doing gymnastics all those years just to get to the Olympics like I thought, but because I loved it so much that it made me feel like I was getting the best out of myself, that it was a part of me and who I was. Nothing or no one could ever change that. That one conversation gave me a whole new outlook on my life and my career. I wasn't going to give up, throw it all away. I was stronger than that. 2005 was an interesting year full of surprises, but a year of coming into my own, on my own, literally. It was just me and my coach now, and being thrust into that number one position was harder than I thought. I had new teammates, a new family.

It wasn't a great year. I was injured with torn ligaments in my ankle, and never really got into shape for the season because of it. My body had changed. I was growing into a young woman, and I was fighting against my curvy Italian genes. The stress of being perfect, of being stick thin and keeping Canada up there in the world rankings was weighing me down. I remember graduating high school with all my girlfriends, and being so relieved that I was starting university, thinking I was done with gymnastics. It was hard to feel that love I once had for the sport, and I was conflicted with wanting to be a normal teenager and not having to compete when I went to university. I had gotten into schools all across Canada, and was ready to follow my friends to London or Kingston. But there was a little snag in my plans. The world championships were coming up in September, a month into university. We needed to finish well to be guaranteed funding from the government the next year, and it all came down to me. It would be my second Worlds. If I wasn't there, our team wasn't developed enough internationally to get the results we needed. I couldn't say no. I decided to go to the University of Toronto on one condition: that I would stay in residence like a normal kid. I wasn't giving up my university experience for a sport that had hurt me so much in the past. I was going to try and have it all, as always.

That first week of September, we had a training camp with all our top Canadian judges and coaches heading to Worlds in the Middle East at the end of the month. Ironically, it was my frosh week at university: a week of stupid debauchery and camp games designed to bring all the new students together and kick off the start of the school year. This is a coveted ritual that high school students literally can't wait for. I had heard stories from my older friends and my sister that this is where you met your group of friends you could cling to during that first scary year on campus. I was not missing frosh week, and I put my foot down. It was then that I made a conscious decision about how I was going to live my life and make it work. I became accustomed to leading a double life, a talent which I had honed over the years and, even until recently, was able to master and keep going. A hidden persona, a secret life, another girl. As I looked in the mirror every morning, the question was always: which Alex would come out to play?

I would be in the gym at 8 a.m., train all day, get back downtown and be ready to go out at 5 or 6 p.m. for whatever we were doing on campus. I was living with six girls in a suite-style dorm. We would go out all night, get home in the early hours of the morning, and with two or three hours of sleep, I would be back in the gym again. I'm not sure how I survived, but I was always good at knowing my body and what it was capable of. I was careful to have the best of both worlds, and even though I knew how important Worlds was—in my head, my experience at the University of Toronto was just as important. I was trying to understand my own motives for training and being in the gym, and needed to figure out exactly what my priorities were. I needed to figure out who I was. I was young and thought I was invincible. When the camp ended and frosh week winded down, I think I slept for three days straight. I loved living downtown and being on my own. It was liberating and exciting, and it was my escape from the gym world that had once consumed all my thoughts. For once I wasn't just Alex the Gymnast. I had found a whole new life that year, one that didn't need sport to feel accepted.

When I left for Worlds, I was happy, really happy for the first time in a long time. That was my first trip to the Middle East, and we barely left the hotel room because we didn't want to go outside. There were no women on the street, and we weren't dressed appropriately. We looked like tourists, out of place, and definitely attracted the wrong kind of attention. I thought to myself that this was it. This would be my last Worlds, and I was at peace with my decision. I didn't tell a soul, but secretly smiled to myself as I soaked in every practice, every moment with my teammates. I really thought that this was the end, and was so happy that I was relaxed when I competed, and had the best competition of the year. I had been off all season, dropping back in the rankings since 2003, really struggling with finding myself. I hadn't been in the top twenty-five all year, and ended up coming in eighteenth overall and making finals. It was all so unexpected. The next day I placed twelfth in one event, and called home to tell my parents the good news. I could hear the excitement in their voices, and a trace of shock maybe as well, but I didn't care as I was completely shocked, along with my coach. We hadn't been working well together all year, our personalities clashing almost daily. We just weren't clicking, but we finally could breathe a sigh of relief. Something had gone right… I knew it was somewhere in there.

Throughout my whole life, I always had a decision to make. It never ended, and not just a little choice either, but a major life-altering decision that would put me down one specific path or another. There were no in-betweens, no maybes. It was a "yes" or a "no". At the time, I had dominated national championships for three years in a row at the senior level, and the second-ranked gymnast was seeded in fortieth or fiftieth place in the world. I knew that Gymnastics Canada didn't want to lose me as I was an asset to them and they needed me. It should have put me in a position of power, but I never really used it. It did help my coach though, and I chose what competitions I wanted to go to and set the plans for our season. No one challenged my coach, and so we each had some decision-making power because of our unique situation. We knew that it was vital I did well for the future of our sport in Canada, and when she came over to my house again, it was like déjà vu with my mom, her and me all sitting in the same kitchen, at the same table, drinking coffee and having "the talk". She knew I was thinking about retiring, and she wanted me to be happy, but I needed to think about my future too. The 2006 Commonwealth Games were coming up, and I had only been to one other multi-sport Games before then: the 2003 Pan American Games where I racked up a few silver and bronze medals behind Sarah. But I was young and didn't understand the prestige and honour of going to a Games and representing your country. I knew it was important, but multi-sport Games are one of the best parts of competing at an elite level in sport. It's your chance to be surrounded by the best of the best, and to meet hundreds of athletes just like you. It's a community, a family, and it was only a few months away. She said, "It's November now, and the Games are in March. You would only have to train for a little while, and could then retire afterwards." I would have a great shot at winning gold, and I knew it. She told me to think about it, but I didn't have to for long. This was my first real opportunity to show the international gymnastics scene that I was still a force to be reckoned with. If I could win the Commonwealth Games, it would be a perfect way to end my career on a high with a personal best in 2005 and an international title in 2006.

I had been targeted as a medal hopeful by CGC, Common-wealth Games Canada, and all of a sudden I was thrown into the spotlight, finding that confidence inside me again. Reporters were calling my house and I was doing media events left, right and centre. I performed at CGC events, and was even asked to model the HBC clothing designed specifically for the Games. It was a big press event, and I stood up on stage with the then president of HBC, George Heller, one of the most inspiring men I had ever met, and had the gall to tell him in front of all the media that I was going to win five gold medals. Years later, he never forgot that. George is a man so invested in Canadian sport, so passionate about our athletes and about providing support for us to achieve our potential. George was and is an inspiration to us all. He understood what we needed as athletes, and he got it. We weren't asking for much more than the respect and resources to train like world-class athletes, to be able to train and compete without worrying about paying rent, eating healthy and paying off loans to travel. George lived, ate, and breathed sport, and he knew that a nation that got behind their athletes was a stronger nation, a healthier nation, and a prouder people. I hope he knows how much he motivated me to stay involved within the athletic community long after I retired. Because of him, I give my time and my life to sport in this country. He is sport in this country to me, and I told him that I was going to bring home all these medals... so cocky! The second it came out of my mouth, I didn't realize the commotion it would cause. All the reporters made a beeline for me, wanting to know all about this arrogant kid from Toronto who was going to sweep the Commonwealth Games. I said it, and so I was going to have to do it, but for some reason it didn't put more pressure on me because this was my goal. If you have a goal, you can't be scared to say it out loud. I put mine out there into the world, it was real, and now it was up to me to go out and get it.

Chapter 3:
My World Record

That winter, I hurt my ankle again and tore ligaments; and sitting on my couch for a few weeks made me gain a lot of weight. It was an uphill battle to get ready for the 2006 Melbourne Games, and I knew that my coach was slipping away from me as though she was embarrassed to have a gymnast that was overweight and out of shape for the rhythmic gymnastics standards. No one wanted to say it, but I could see it on their faces. A month before the Games, they came down on me hard, and it was disastrous. They told me that for a normal girl, my body was fine, but in the gym world it wasn't going to cut it. A recommendation to join Jenny Craig made me laugh hysterically with tears streaming down my cheeks. I was an 18-year-old girl at a healthy weight, and directed to diets and places that could help me with my "problem". I was disgusted with everyone around me, and didn't have a single productive training session up until the day I competed in Melbourne. I not only drove myself insane, but everyone around me too. My coach didn't know what to do with me, my teammates couldn't help, and no one understood what I was going through. I had to do it on my own, like I was used to doing.

Melbourne was one of the greatest experiences of my life. Even though I was crumbling inside, I got on the plane at Toronto Pearson International Airport and smiled. I had never been to Australia, and here I was, going to represent my country. I wanted to meet other athletes and have fun, and was glad to get away from Toronto where I was so stressed. With my two teammates in tow, Yana and Carly, we flew from Toronto to L.A., and then to Auckland and Melbourne. Thirty-six hours later, delirious and exhausted, we arrived at the athlete village. You could tell we were rhythmics: glammed up coming off the plane with huge suitcases. We lugged all our clothes, way too much stuff, to our tiny room in a huge house we shared with three different sports teams, only to find another suitcase filled with HBC Canada gear. We broke down in laughter. Our room was incredibly hot, and we were basically living on top of each other. Being the last to arrive, we got the smallest room, but we didn't care. The house was huge, and there were other gymnasts, squash and soccer players living co-ed among the rooms. That first day, we got the day off and explored the village, and got settled in. Training started on the following day, and because we only competed the last three days of the Games, there would be a gruelling wait ahead of us. What a trip that was. All three of us could not train to save our lives, and it was the worst we had ever looked. Our coaches reamed us out in front of all the other countries training. It was embarrassing. Here were the Canadians, the gold medal hopefuls, the competition—and we were awful. Our coaches made us train twice a day, sometimes staying at the gym in between because there wasn't enough time to go back to the village. We were praying for some sort of miracle. All the colour left our faces, and we were pale, tired, rundown and nervous. Other athletes that we became friends with took us in, and took our minds off it all, and the Opening Ceremonies brought our spirits up. I had never been to one before, none of us had. It was incredible, and I got a taste of what the Olympics must feel like. The stadium was packed full of thousands and thousands of people, a glistening ball of camera flashes. The Queen declared the 2006 Commonwealth Games officially open, and the fireworks display was the best I've ever seen. Acrobats on roller skates with sparklers shooting out of their backs, spun all around us. It was beautiful, and I looked beside me at my teammates and knew how special this was and what this meant for our sport back home. We threw our arms around each other and stood there side by side soaking in the moment. This was our time. After watching different sports bring back medals to the village and celebrate over the first week, it was finally our turn to compete, and we knew what we had to do. All of a sudden it all clicked into place. The three of us, with our scores combined, won the Team Gold that first day by a long margin. We stood on top of that podium, together as a team, and celebrated not just the medal hanging around our necks, but what we went through to get there: the fears, the frustrations, and the fight. The next day, I won the overall gold medal, becoming the 2006 Commonwealth Games Champion. I sang the Canadian National Anthem and watched them raise our flag ever so slowly in front of thousands of people on their feet. I could hear my mom in the stands screaming for me, and it was all worth it to stand there in that moment. Each day that we came back to the village, Team Canada would be there cheering us on. Most of the sports were done, and came to watch us or sat in front of the big screens they had up in the village displaying our competition. They were all behind us, and that last day was mine for the taking.

It was event finals and the Canadian media knew I could take four gold. The way the finals worked was that we would compete in one event and have the medal ceremony, then compete again and have the medal ceremony, for all four events. One gold medal after another, I stood up on that podium and listened to my national anthem. As I stood there waiting to compete in my last event, with five gold medals in my bag, everyone knew this could be a historical moment. No one had ever won six gold before. I stepped foot into the stadium for the last time and slowly walked up the steps to the carpet on a raised platform in the middle of this huge arena. I can still remember the feel of the carpet on my feet, wiping the sweat off my hands as I threw my towel down beside me, and the buzzing sounds of a hushed audience. Every person there knew my name, and I went out for the last time and have never had so much fun competing. I was flying. My mom and Yana's mom had flown down for four days just to watch us, and I could hear them on their feet. My breath, their breath. I finished that last event and took my time walking off the carpet. The packed stadium erupted with applause on their feet. I waved to my fans and didn't want to walk off as I never wanted to forget that feeling, the electricity coursing through my veins. Even the volunteers at the venue were crying for me, patting me on the back, taking pictures and breathing a sigh of relief when my score came up. When I won that last gold medal, they announced that I had broken a world record for my sport, and that I had also tied the world record for most golds ever won by a single athlete at a Games. It was unbelievable. An out-of-body experience. I sang the national anthem for the last time as I tried to remember every detail of that moment, every goose bump. They weren't supposed to do this, but as I was leaving the gym for the last time, one of the volunteers gave me the Canadian flag that was raised six times for me. The press had a field day. I was chosen to be Canada's flag bearer for the Closing Ceremonies that night, an honour that will stay in my heart forever. Holding that flag, I knew my life had taken an unexpected twist, and this was my destiny. I walked slowly around the stadium as we said goodbye to Melbourne, leading hundreds of Canadian athletes behind me. I couldn't have been more proud to be Canadian in that moment. It was then that I knew I couldn't give up on the Olympics. I wouldn't have been able to live with myself if I let it pass me by without trying. It was a part of who I was. And it was then that getting to Beijing in two years became my only focus.

Chapter 4:
The Olympian

lightened my course load at university, and sat down with my coach to plan for Beijing. That's what I wanted, and I knew she could take me there. No matter how difficult it was going to be and how hard she was going to push me, this was what I wanted. I knew exactly what I was getting myself into, and I was hungry again. The only thing we could do was get out there and compete, hit up the world cup circuit, go to training camps alongside the world champions in Eastern Europe, train more hours, sacrifice normal twenty-something living and stay in when everyone was going out and having fun.

My weight became a huge concern, and I began to workout with a trainer and put all my energy into getting into shape. I would have done anything to slim down. Olympic qualifiers were in September 2007, and I had a little over a year to put everything I had towards that one day. It meant everything to me. No one was going to stand in my way, and I didn't let them.

2007 started off with a bang. I was sent off to Moscow to train without my coach for a few weeks in their national centre. I was terrified. I didn't speak a word of Russian, and I knew how difficult it was going to be, how the training was going to make me feel the worst I had ever felt. I knew what to expect, but it still didn't prepare me for the actual camp. Pain doesn't begin to describe it. The exertion, the sweat, the blood. Now it was clear why the Russians were the best in the world because they trained like this every day of their lives since they were little girls. They didn't have school, or work or family to deal with to occupy their time.

They had one thing to do and one thing only. No distractions. I improved more at that camp than I did in the whole of 2004. The Americans were also training there at the same time, and their national champion was vying for that Olympic spot as well. She was my direct competition, and it helped me to train alongside her, to see how she worked, to see her attitude in the gym and the type of person she was. They had their whole team and their coaches there, while I was all alone. There were days when I longed for my coach, for some familiarity, some real concern or love, just a hand on my back, some warm words of encouragement. But they weren't there. I became so strong. I would close my eyes and wipe the sweat dripping down my face, feel my muscles shaking and the burn from my knees as they bled through my tights. All I could think of was Beijing. All I could see was the Olympics. "Just keep going, it will all be over soon, don't stop. Please just don't stop." I begged my body to listen. Sometimes it didn't, but that constant fight between mind, body and soul kept me moving.

It was a great competitive year for me. I was in the best shape of my life. Finally the hours in the gym, combined with stress and the discipline I had, were paying off. I had lost weight, and was light and fast. Everyone noticed, and I had an energy about myself that I hadn't had in years. It felt right. It was going to happen. All I had left was the Pan American Games in Brazil at the end of July, and then Olympic Qualifiers in September. That's it, it was finally here and I was so ready for it, I wasn't even nervous. But nothing was ever easy for me, and it was all too good to be true.

I headed down to Brazil with my best friend and teammate, Stef. Yana and Carly had retired, and with a hard goodbye I knew that they were with me in spirit. Stef began training with my coach that year after switching clubs, and we instantly became close. She was probably the funniest girl I have ever trained with, and she could always make me smile with her huge laugh. Stef had improved so much that year, and I couldn't have been happier to have her on my team. We were quite the pair, and walked into that gym and made it known that we were a team to watch. My coach had it easy this time as we were both so on. Sharp and energized, we were ready to compete, and I was both anxious and impatient to get out there. My coach would always laugh at me when I was like that as she knew this meant I was confident and prepared. She could breathe a little easier then.

The competition was spread over three days, and the first day was qualifying for the all around, so only the top ten moved through. The second day was where we would duke it out for the Pan Am title; and the third day was event finals, which would take the top eight finishers in each event from the first day of competition. Confusing I know. It was the first day, and I couldn't have felt better. I had competed in two events and was far ahead of the American. We were ecstatic. I figured it would be close, but I didn't expect to be that far ahead. I was a shoe in for gold, but it was still qualifying round, so we didn't get too ahead of ourselves. It was my third event, and I marched out there with my ribbon in hand, so confident. I was the crowd favourite, and I could feel their energy and thrived on it. Halfway through my routine, the impossible happened. My ribbon broke in half. The metal swivel that holds the stick to the ribbon completely detached, and I couldn't get it back together. I couldn't hear the crowd, the music, my coach. I was in a daze but didn't even think of stopping. That wasn't in my nature. Within a split second all these thoughts were running through my head, and I gathered up my ribbon and kept going without my apparatus. If I was going down, I was going down in my own style, in my own way. I finished and sat there, motionless, stunned on the carpet. The crowd was on its feet, erupting in applause. I was in complete shock. The judges were in shock. No one knew what to do. I slowly walked off, not sure of what just happened, or what it meant. I still can't put words to what was going on inside me the moment it happened, the sharp intake of breathe, the screaming inside my head; and I only kept moving on instinct.

The scoreboard flashed a zero, and I broke down in tears as the thousands of people in the stands started to boo the judges loud enough to shake the arena. They wanted this for me, and tears streamed down the faces of those I passed as I couldn't bear to look anymore. I could see the Canadian judges fighting with the head judge. My coach got me out of there quickly and told me that I had one more event to do. "Just focus," she said, "they only take three scores to go into the overall competition. Don't worry. Stop crying." This was a lie that we both needed to believe at the time. I don't remember doing anything until it was my last event. I went out there and don't remember how my last event even went. I don't remember coming off the carpet or seeing my score. I was still in shock. If I had had a spare ribbon on the side of the carpet I would have been fine. I would have picked it up and gotten a deduction for substituting a piece of apparatus, but I wouldn't have gotten a zero. Apparently, if you are not halfway through your routine when your ribbon breaks, you get an automatic zero. We fought that I was halfway through, but the decision was already made by the head judge. My zero would stand. I ended up eleventh with three scores: a few tenths of a point off the tenth place to squeeze into the all around the next day. I was basically disqualified, and couldn't believe this was happening to me. I came back to the village and was a different person. Everyone had seen what had happened. They were watching it on YouTube by the time I was back in my room—the whole Canadian team was aware that I had been disqualified, that the title I wanted, the dream of being Pan American champion, was gone. I went to the cafeteria and ate dinner, fuming. I was so angry I put my fork through the Styrofoam plate and dented the table. No one would talk to me. It was deadly quiet all around me, with everyone whispering behind my back but too scared to approach me. I couldn't even look at myself in the mirror. Stef was competing the next day and had a shot for a medal, but I didn't want to go and watch someone else take the title that I knew could have been mine. Yet I knew that I had to support her, and I wanted her to do well, so I sucked up my pride, my hurt and my anger, and I went the next day and watched the entire competition. Stef did so well despite having had to deal with me as a roommate and the disappointment of our entire team, and I was so proud of her. I trained in the back while they were finishing up, putting everything I had in me out on the carpet. All the volunteers sat and watched me. I had become Brazil's sweetheart: the human interest story of the Games. Everyone backed me and supported me. They were with me, and I can't quite describe what that feels like to have a community of people that don't know you at all, rally behind you and believe in you. It was so powerful, and it gave me the strength to stand tall.

I was still eligible to compete in three finals the next day, and I wanted gold… and that's exactly what I got: three gold medals. The Canadian national anthem played three times in a row, but I wasn't happy; and as horrible as that is to admit, I wanted five. And I knew I could have had them. Another athlete and a friend of mine had to knock some sense into me, which I desperately needed, and I thank him for that. He told me how incredible it was to just have one gold, let alone three. "Snap out of it, grow up and be proud of yourself," he said. Some athletes only dream of doing what I did. When I took the blinders off and stepped out of the gymnastics bubble, I got it. I saw what I had done, and the accomplishment that it really was. I was the most decorated athlete at the Games, and was asked to be Canada's flag bearer again at the Closing Ceremonies. It put so much into perspective for me. So it was just a title, so what! In the end, what did that matter? I knew what I had done, and I was in the best shape of my career, the most skilled and consistent. When had anything ever been easy for me? This was my time.

World Championships were held that year in a little town in Greece called Patras. After the emotional whirlwind of Brazil, I wanted to compete more before I would try and qualify for the Olympics for the last time. We ended up setting up a six-week trip that would take me to Slovenia, Germany and Bulgaria for three world cups and a training camp before I set foot in the Mediterranean. My teammates Stef and Ali met me in Germany.

Those six weeks were perfect for me. I was making finals at world cups, consistently in the top fifteen, and training well. Maybe after all this time, this was really my Games, and not Athens. By the time we got to Greece, we were a well-oiled machine. Our hotel overlooked the water, and the cool breeze coming in off the waves brought a calming feeling to all of us. This was my third world championships, and I knew what to expect. I knew the people, the teams, and the competition. I was a veteran now, no longer that young girl, the up and coming gymnast learning as she went. I was now teaching the others.

I knew how things were going to go, and I could go through the motions without nerves creeping up. We competed one event per day, and after the fourth day, the top twenty would qualify for the Beijing Olympics. All our parents decided to make the trip to see us, and it could have been the last time for all of us that we were out there. This was a special trip, one they didn't want to miss. After the first few days, things were looking good, but I knew all too well that one day could make the biggest difference, and things could slip out of your hands within a blink of an eye. I was in my element, and performed to the best of my ability; and that's all I could do. It was the highlight of my career. I sat in the kiss and cry with my coach after my last routine, where you wait with cameras in your face to see your score, ready to capture your most personal reaction. I was near the end of the pack this time as everyone else had finished competing, and my ranking would tell us if I was in or not. When the score came up, I went into complete shock. I couldn't see my name, and in a fit of panic I turned to my coach frantically: "Why couldn't I see my name?" But I was looking too far down. "Look up," she said. I had placed ninth overall, and had not only qualified for the Olympics as the only North or South American athlete, but finished in the top ten—something no other Canadian gymnast had done in 24 years. It was a surreal moment. Nothing else mattered after that. I had done it. We had done it. My coach embraced me and I could feel her heart beating out of her chest. She was so happy. Four years of heartbreak came pouring out of me. Everyone was crying tears of happiness and relief all around me. I had finally done it, put Canada on the map in a way that hadn't been done in so long, and I showed girls everywhere that you don't have to be a size 0 to make it in this sport. You don't have to kill yourself and your body to gain respect from your competitors. You can be strong and lean and muscular. You can be your own person, and be different. When I was younger I was told I would never make it as a rhythmic gymnast, that I didn't have the right body type, I was too big. I was talented, but would never make it to the Olympic level. "Give up and try something else," that person would say. I think back to that person now and smile. No matter how many times people don't believe in you, if you believe in yourself, you can break down barriers. You can make a change. My sport wasn't used to gymnasts like me, but I made them all accept me. I didn't let it break me. It hurt to be seen as different for so many years, fighting against who I am; but in the end, I wouldn't change one thing. If I showed one young girl that she can be anything she wants to be, then it was all worth it. You don't have to look like the women in magazines to get ahead, to find love, to be happy. You can be yourself. Love yourself, and anything can happen.

We celebrated all night long, and it's a memory that I can still see so vividly. Team Canada ate dinner at this beautiful restaurant outside on the water, with music and wine flowing all evening. We all over-indulged. We could relax. I was going to the Olympics; Canada was going to the Olympics. All I wanted to do was jump up and down on my bed and scream at the top of my lungs, but I didn't get to celebrate for too long. The very next day I was in meetings with our national team advisor and my coach, making plans for Beijing. So now the goal was to make the final and finish in the top ten. The plans were all set in motion, and felt like they were going ahead without me. I was stuck in Greece, and I wanted to stay there. I had never imagined what it would actually be like if I had qualified. What that would mean? What was going to happen? It all suddenly caught up to me so quickly about the responsibility I had as North America's only Olympian in my sport, and it brought with it so much more pressure into my life.

I wish I could look back on that year and say it was the best year of my life. I wish I could say that I had the fairytale Olympic experience. But I can't. Deep down I know that things in your life happen for a reason no matter how discouraging or dark. But for a long time I couldn't believe how unfair things had turned out for me. Within a few short weeks, my life turned upside down again. One thing I have learned through all of this is that the unexpected and the unfair can happen at any time. When you don't want things to change, that's when they do. You have to learn to adapt and pick yourself up as fast as you can. There's sometimes nothing you can do about it but accept it and move on. Figure out a new game plan, a way of making something out of it you never thought possible. If I've learned anything at all from my life in sport it's that things don't happen the way you want them to. You don't get everything you want, and just because you worked hard doesn't mean someone else isn't better. Life can be brutally harsh, but it's how you deal with it that matters. It's how you deal with it that makes you the type of person you are.

When we all got back from Greece and the dust had settled, my coach gave me some pretty big news. She was moving to Spain. This was something that had been in the works for a while, a position that she couldn't turn down. In Canada there is no national team coach position, no salary. She was surviving and supporting herself on what her gymnasts paid her. Money was always a problem, and coaching was never as glamorous as I always thought it was. My parents needed a whole extra salary just to cover my costs, including how we were going to fund my coach to travel with me, and who was going to pay for what. The little funding that we received from the Federal Government barely covered a plane ticket per month. I would get a cheque for $1,500 every month, which would not even cover the cost of two competitive gym suits. I had about four to six a year, not to mention the plane tickets to Europe for myself, my coach, and my

Breaking Through My Limits

judge. This amounted to a career that could cost up to $60,000 a year. That $1,500 was looking pretty small then. I would rely on grants and charities to help my family out, so I understood why my coach had to go. I understood, but I couldn't help but feel lost. She was treated like a queen over in Spain, given an apartment near the beach, a car, and an incredible facility to train the girls. As much as I didn't want things to change and to see her go, she had to. I was only going to be around until the Olympics, and she had her whole life to think of afterwards. She is without a doubt one of the greatest coaches in the world, so it looked like I was to pack my bags and head to Spain. Training in Toronto by myself or with other coaches wasn't working. I wasn't pushing myself, and a new coach would never want to change your style or your routines, especially a gymnast at my level, because they wouldn't want to interfere. So I just coasted along until I got to Spain to stay with my coach, but it put my development back more than we ever figured it would. I think everyone was telling themselves that this arrangement would work, that everything would be fine. But it wouldn't be. She couldn't be at every competition with me because of her new job and the responsibilities that came with it. I ended up being passed around from coach to coach, and it was awkward and uncomfortable for me. And then the worst happened. I was nowhere near the shape I was in a few short months ago when I qualified for the Olympics. I was slower, not as sharp, off my game. I just needed to focus and get back to that discipline, find that drive and edge, and she was the only one that could bring it out in me.

In February I was at my first competition of the season in Portugal, with five months until the Olympic Opening Ceremonies. I was finishing up my last event when I went to launch myself into a turning jump with my body arched backwards. I slipped on takeoff, but my body was already starting to go through the motions without the air height, and I landed on my ankle, cracking it. I fell to the floor and I couldn't move. I was paralyzed, and the pain was unbearable. I lay there in the middle of the floor in front of hundreds of people, and the reaction of the dead silent crowd summoned a paramedic. I tried to get up but couldn't stand. My ankle bone was lifeless, and I thought I had broken it. The fear that washed over me was unbearable. In a few seconds, I may have just given up the last seventeen years of my life. They rushed me to the hospital with our national team advisor, but not my coach. She wasn't there. I was so scared and alone but didn't want to show it. The hospital was filled with the moans of people in pain and a smell that I will never be able to express in words. People with blood all over them sat beside me in trauma. I had to get out of there. I wrapped up my ankle by myself and got on the first flight home to Toronto, straight to the best sports doctor we knew in the city. I had to fly back completely by myself carrying all my bags on my broken ankle. It was one of the worst experiences of my life. No one to help me, no crutches, every limp was filled with pain, making me sick to my stomach. Dragging my bags behind me, every inch took enough strength to move a mountain. I didn't think I was going to make it, and I was so lucky that I squeezed in to see this doctor back home as he was doing me a favour, and I owe him my life. I have never been so scared than I was those few months. I had to be able to compete in Beijing, that wasn't an option. I was going to the Olympics. I had come so far, I wasn't going to sit by and watch someone take my spot again. The hardest part was keeping positive, but that was a struggle I fought every day, some days coming out victorious, and some breaking my heart. As he examined my ankle for the first time, he pressed into my torn ligaments and my whole body broke out in a sweat, with my face going beet red. He pushed in repeatedly to find out how many I had torn, and how badly I had torn them, and my body reacted to his touch, fighting my gag reflex. He let go and told me I had torn three ligaments and needed to be in treatment every day. I told him I would do anything, just fix me. He smiled and promised me he would.

The next few weeks I couldn't train. I couldn't do anything. I lived in the clinic. I did physio, acupuncture, and all different kinds of treatments, trying anything that might help. There was an ice bath permanently attached to my body, which I carried around with me. Every time someone new would come in and see my ankle, their eyes would open wide, and I could see what was going on in their mind: there's no way she's competing at the Olympics. I refused to believe it. If I didn't compete all year I'd be fine; and as long as I had two months, I could get ready for the Games. It didn't matter how I was going to compete now, it was just being able to compete. Ironically enough, I met the greatest people while I was in rehab, like Ohenewa Akuffo, a female wrestler healing up for the Games, Perdita Felicien, the Canadian hurdling queen, and Nicole Forrester, high jump Olympian. All these women were so strong and so positive that I couldn't help but feel inspired. We spent almost every day together that summer, and if it wasn't for them, I don't know if I would have found the strength to make it through this. To not have my coach by my side helping me through it was horrible enough. She was so far away, and I couldn't even imagine telling her what I had done. I didn't want her to know, and couldn't bear to see how distraught she would be. Everything that was so right the year before had suddenly become so wrong. I had everyone I knew praying for me. I missed all the major tournaments, and wasn't even able to compete at my last national championships. It was awful. I couldn't even tell people how bad my injury was because I didn't want to spark rumours that maybe I shouldn't be going to the Games after all. It was not how I expected my last year in the sport to be at all, to never compete in front of a home crowd again, and not to have a proper goodbye to the community that I loved so much. It broke my heart, but I had to tell myself that it was all a test, a test to see how strong I was. If I got through this, I could get through anything. Sure enough, my ankle was getting better, where I could tape it up so tightly that my ligaments were held together, and I could get back into the gym. The pain would always be there and I had to accept that, but as long as it stayed in one piece I could train. I was alone though: no coach, no supervision. That first week, I was pushing it a little more every day and was gaining confidence. I decided to start jumping, and on one of my first attempts, sprained my other ankle. I collapsed to the floor and screamed out to no one. I was alone, and crawled to the phone thinking that this was it, it was all over. Every inch that I slid closer to the phone, the pain pierced through my ankle and up my legs. I willed myself to stop panicking as it was getting harder and harder for me to breathe. The panic in my voice oozed out of me, and I didn't even sound like myself. I called my doctor and he told me to come in immediately, so I bandaged myself up with whatever I had and somehow drove to the clinic. His face said it all. It was a sprain. I either had the worst luck, or someone didn't want me to go to the Olympics. Treatment after treatment, I would stay there for countless hours on end until I could finally get back into the gym with both ankles now taped and cutting off the circulation to my calves. But I didn't care, and I made sure not to jump until a few weeks before the Olympics. I didn't even train full-out until I competed. It was all a big secret that no one even knew, all an elaborate ruse to make sure that the judges didn't catch wind that I was hurt, or else it could damage their opinion of me coming into the Olympics. I wouldn't be seen as a contender anymore.

The second I could train again, I was on a plane to Spain to be with my coach, but I was in so much pain that I could barely walk when I took the tape off. It was the worst pain of my life. I would run ice cold baths and keep my feet permanently in them, closing my eyes and praying I would step out and be miraculously cured. I'd dream of waking up and jumping out of bed being able to walk without a limp. She came back to Toronto for a month so I could be at home with my family and my teammates while I prepared for the moment I had been waiting for over the past seventeen years. I just never thought it would be in this way; that I would be in a medical clinic more than the actual gym. But that's life, no sense in crying about it. I did what I had to do. We did a little test run right before the Olympics at a small competition in Bulgaria, and I was cautious, but it was good to get out there and compete again.

It went surprisingly well, better than I thought, and it gave me my confidence back. I could survive, I could do this, and I travelled with my beautiful teammate Demi for that last competition, that last leg of my career. I don't know if she realizes what a special time that was for me, but it was an end of an era. She was so young and so full of promise and potential. I hope that I helped to show her that she could do whatever she set her mind to, that you could be different and still excel, and you could laugh in the face of the impossible. She took my mind off my injuries, and we had so much fun together. We laughed and cried, and had the most ridiculous conversations. I needed her with me for support, and I will always thank her for coming all the way from Vancouver to train and compete for one last competition of the season that she didn't really have to. She took time out of her preparation for the next year to be with me, to help me gain back my confidence. Keep smiling love. You are so beautiful inside and out.

Then it was finally time. I remember the day before my flight to China. I was sitting in my living room with my mom packing, and was so excited that I couldn't stop talking. It was happening. Finally my dream was coming true. I must have pinched myself a million times to make sure I was awake, and if I could have run with my ankles, I would have run all the way to the gate in the airport. My coach and I wore our Canada jackets proudly as we boarded the 747 heading straight to Beijing, and my mom took pictures of us walking through security. The next time she would see me I would be competing at the Olympic Games. I remember thinking that I must have been living a dream. This couldn't actually be happening... but it was.

From that moment on, I was in heaven. From the very first step outside the airport in Beijing, the humidity hit me, and I knew I had arrived. The sweat dripped down by back, and my hair began to curl in the heat. Even though I had been to multi-sport Games before, nothing compared to the feeling of driving up to the athlete village for the first time, to see the Olympic rings everywhere, and to wear your accreditation around your neck, proudly branded an

Olympian. Nothing could get me down now, no injury, no bad training. The village was like a city with its own buses and streets weaving around all the apartment buildings and facilities. There was everything you could have imagined at our fingertips: a gym, a training pool, a leisure pool, a shopping mall, international zone, video game lounges, Internet lounges, meeting places, pool rooms, and basketball nets. There was a river running through it, and beautiful, decorative pieces and sculptures everywhere you turned. It felt like we were in China, but in our own little world. The cafeteria was the biggest I've ever seen, open 24 hours with more food than we would ever need. I stayed far away from the McDonald's until after I was done competing. Everything was so organized and well run, and I felt like I was staying in a resort not an athletes' village. I lucked out and stayed in a three-person suite in which two girls opted to stay out of the village to focus, so I had this huge room to myself the entire Games. It was perfect. I immediately draped my huge Canadian flag over my balcony and hit the streets to explore. You could rent bikes during the day, and ride around and get out into the city to clear your head. I loved every second of my Olympic experience, even with two taped ankles. My coach and I were so relaxed because up until a month ago there was a very real possibility that we wouldn't even be here. We were celebrating in our own right. It was a miracle. Every day before training I would get my ankles taped up by the medical centre, and my physio team became my family. I had one very special woman travel with me to and from the venues, making sure I had everything I needed. She was a miracle worker. Without her I never would have felt as comfortable as I did with all that tape on, holding my ankles together. She took away as much pain as she could, and I will be forever grateful for that.

After a few days of acclimatization it was finally Opening Ceremonies. This was the moment that I had been waiting for my entire life. When I was a little girl, I would stay up and watch the opening ceremonies of the Olympics live, wherever they were in the world. I knew that I was going to be one of those people out on the track, that I would be an athlete. And here I was seventeen years later, realizing my dream. I was going to be one of the people that I used to idolize, and maybe even inspire future athletes sitting at home in Canada, watching us walk behind our flag. All I remember wanting to know so badly was how the track felt under my feet, and what it sounded like to walk on it. For years I imagined the sensation. My whole body was tingling with excitement. We were ushered into the arena besides the Bird's Nest (the main stadium), and sat there with all the other countries, waiting for our turn to make the long, slow walk to the main stadium where we would finally have our moment. It felt like hours to wait, and the energy was infectious. Each country would be called to start lining up and heading over. Finally, it was Canada's turn. The heat was unbearable as thousands of athletes were crammed all together in a gigantic line outside that weaved its way towards the stadium. We could hear the crowd and the performers as we got closer and closer. Team Canada was wearing white, and in the heat it was all turning see-through. No one anticipated that we would be standing outside in the humidity for hours, but there were no complaints. It was the Opening Ceremonies of the Olympic Games. This was what we had dreamed of. We got to a waiting spot where they handed out food and water, and the anticipation was draining us as it felt like we would never get there. And then the sights and sounds were so close you got goose bumps. The opening to the arena was just in front of us, and it was our turn next. It looked like we were going into a dark tunnel before emerging in the middle of the madness. It got quiet all of a sudden when we entered the building, as if we all knew it was coming. Then without media cameras, without any other countries, without anyone but Team Canada, someone started singing "O Canada" in the dark. It was so raw and beautiful that we all joined in. It was just us in that moment, so proud to be Canadian, so honoured, so inspired. No matter what happened, no matter if you won a medal or not, whether you had the performance of your lifetime or you didn't, we could all sleep at night knowing we were a part of this team.

Together we were strong, we were one. When we walked out into the spotlight, we knew that we'd never get a moment like that all together again, and it is something that I will hold in my heart forever.

Walking out after the moment they called "Canada," put my senses on fire. I didn't want to miss a single thing. I wanted to soak in every last detail. It was better than I could have ever imagined, and the sheer size of the stadium made me feel like I was two feet tall with the tens of thousands of people on their feet cheering, snapping photos. The lights were all on us, and we were the main attraction. The feeling in the air, my teammates' expressions, the whistling and yelling coming from all directions—you almost didn't want to take pictures because you wanted to see it all with your own eyes. My mouth hung open as I struggled not to be in awe of what was happening all around me. And as long as it took to get there, was the opposite of how quickly it was over. We were ushered into the middle of the stadium, and free to run around and do whatever we wanted. We interacted with other countries and watched the rest of the nations march in. I closed my eyes and just felt the pounding beat of the music and the buzz of people beside me. The memory is still so fresh as if it was yesterday. There was a CBC camera up in the press box shooting down on us, and I was given a phone and did an interview as they zoomed in from the top of the stadium. My mom told me I better get on camera somehow, and I did Mom, see. It couldn't have been more perfect, and it was only right then that I felt like an Olympian.

I wish the two weeks hadn't flown by as fast as they did, but it was over so quickly. All those years of waiting and training and hoping, and then it comes and goes as if it was never even there. I competed almost at the very end of the whole thing, like usual, and it was hard to train the first week as the media was coming down on all our athletes for not winning medals. To hear your own country put your team down was unbearable, and so disappointing to see them turn against us. When we finally won that first gold medal, everything started to flow a bit better. People relaxed a bit more, and the pressure started to lift. The second week we were on a high. The media was back on our side, and we picked up momentum. You could definitely feel it when you woke up in the morning, and it was so clear whether or not it was a good day or a bad one for our team, even from sitting on the main floor in our athlete's lounge. The air was filled with tension that you could cut with a knife. All I knew was that I was having the time of my life. My coach and I both knew that I wasn't going for a medal. I had competed once all year, so if I made it through with four consistent, clean routines, this would be the best ending we could hope for. So we were both more relaxed than we had ever been at a competition together. We went to the markets and she gave me a day off, not pushing my body like we used to. I took care of my ankles really well, and the night before my competition we decided to go see my parents outside the village. I usually would never do that, but they were as much a part of this journey as I was, and I needed to see them. I got out of the taxi and saw my parents, my aunt, uncle and my sister standing on the street. They ran to me, my sister jumping on me, almost knocking me over on the sidewalk, with the locals thinking we were insane. We went to Canada Olympic House, the safe haven for all Canadian friends and family of the athletes, and sat outside and celebrated. We were here, tomorrow, no matter what, we were still here. Seventeen years of gymnastics, and we had made it. We were at the Olympic Games.

The next day I was the first competitor to compete, just my luck. I hated going first, and everyone knew it, but I had to smile because, of course, the one time I was first in the last few years, it would be at the Olympics. I remember walking towards the competition arena from the practice gym. It was a two-minute walk, and you followed a woman who led you there. My coach was behind me and was just as nervous as I was; and then we got to these big double doors. The woman in front of me stepped to the side, and they opened up in front of me. With a gust of wind, I could hear the crowd, see the shine of the bright lights, and feel the energy change. For a split second I wanted to turn around and run. The whole world was watching. It hit me that in a minute I would be competing at the Olympic Games; and nothing could have prepared me for that. I took a deep breath, turned to look at my coach, and stepped into the arena, standing there waiting for the green flag to go up, the signal that the judges were ready, and for the announcer to call my name. My coach put her hands on my shoulders. I was doing this for me, for her, for my family, for anyone that supported me. I closed my eyes and squeezed them shut. This was it. I went out there, and all the pain was gone. We didn't care about scores; we knew what I had done to get there.

Heading into the second day, I was sitting in fifteenth, which wasn't where I would have wanted to be, but that wasn't the issue anymore. For me, it was about competing and getting out there, showing everyone that you can survive the impossible; that you can come back from anything. That next day I did my hair for the last time, applied my makeup, and stared at myself in the mirror. I remember being calmer than I had ever been. My fingers weren't shaking as I packed up my bag, and I looked back over my shoulder into my room as I left, and remember thinking that the next time I would be in that room, it would be all over. My family was sitting in the stands wearing their "Team Alex" shirts, with a Canadian flag draped around their shoulders. They had flown halfway around the world for me, and it was all coming to an end now. A huge banner was draped over the side of the stands with my name on it from a Canadian family that had travelled halfway around the world to see me. In a few short hours I would be sitting back in this room having competed at my first Olympics, and my last competition ever. I needed a moment to gather my thoughts. I thought of the little girl that was told she would never be good enough. I thought of the girl who was told she was too fat to make it to the Olympics. I thought of the woman who was strong enough to battle back. I thought about the injuries and the stress I put on my body. And I thought about all the sacrifices everyone had made for me. I saw my family. This was for them. I taped up my ankles and went out there for the last time. I heard my name being called: "Alexandra Orlando, Canada". The Canadian flag was next to my name on the scoreboard, and I felt the carpet underneath my feet and heard the sound of my breath before the music started, and the hush of the crowd for that millisecond before I would start moving. And then I played.

The judges' eyes were on me, and it was over as fast as it had begun. I heard the cheering, I waved to the crowd, but inside I didn't know what to feel, I could barely smile. I made one mistake in my final event and felt so discouraged, so upset as I walked off. I tried so hard not to be, to tell myself to enjoy that I was done, to enjoy this incredible moment, and that I had put it all out there and should have no regrets. But I couldn't help it, it wasn't perfect. I dropped from fifteenth place, and my coach told me to stop being upset and smile, and that I was done. But I couldn't. The cameras were in front of me and I was scared that if I tried to smile I would break down in tears. I'm not sure if it was the mistake or the fact that I was done and it wasn't the competition of my lifetime. It wasn't Worlds, which was still the highlight of my career. Nothing would ever top that. I guess I had an idea of what Beijing was going to be like, and it wasn't that. We all imagine things a certain way sometimes, and watch it play out in our heads, expecting to feel a certain way. But this wasn't a Cinderella story. As I walked through the mixed zone, there were a million cameras calling girls names and asking for their comments; and the Canadian media wanted me. A very good friend of mine, a reporter for CBC sports, called me over and asked about my family and what it felt like to have them there. I lost it. I could barely speak, choking back tears. I knew that I owed everything to them in that moment. Having them there with me meant more than anything in the world. I never wanted to disappoint them, and I thought I had. My parents would kill me for thinking this, but it's true. I stood there under the bright lights with a microphone in my face, and I told them I loved them. And I knew that they would always love me regardless of if I won a medal or not, and they were so proud of me. I wiped away the tears and kept moving through the zone, getting pulled for one more interview. Lights, camera, action: "Alexandra, how does it feel to not live up to expectations?" I felt like I got punched in the stomach, and took one look at this little man, so tempted to punch him in the face, and smiled instead. I had to laugh, "I don't live up to anyone's expectations but my own," I said, and walked away, out of the gym and out of that world forever. And as I walked away I realized that I believed that. I went back to the village immediately, but couldn't face my family yet. I needed to be upset. I needed to get my frustration out. I had so many emotions running through my body that I needed to be on my own. I needed to cry if I wanted to. I needed to take a burning hot shower and sing at the top of my lungs, and I needed to be around athletes who were going through what I was. My family thought I could do no wrong, and I know I should have been happy, but my career was over in a way that I didn't choose or have control over. I didn't have a say in the matter. I was injured and couldn't compete to my best ability, and now it was over, no redemption, no second chance. Not the fairytale ending every little athlete dreams of; but perfection was never the name of the game for me. I went to the Closing Ceremonies and celebrated with my team. All that passion, all that frustration, it was all exposed. When my family flew home, I stayed in China.

When those final days wound down and everyone was packing up and leaving, I sent my suitcases home and I flew to Shanghai and Hong Kong. I needed the trip to be on my own, to stay in a hotel and tour unknown cities, and to be practically invisible. I didn't have to talk to anyone; I didn't have to do anything. I wanted to avoid the post-Olympic syndrome once you got home and were faced with a million questions. I needed a break, and I needed it all to blow over. I had to get ready for the next phase of my life, the next chapter where everything was going to be different, and I needed to let that sink in. For the last seventeen years, all I knew was rhythmic gymnastics, which was as much a part of my life as breathing. It wasn't all that I was, but it had made me the woman I had become. It had given me such highs and lows that I didn't know if I would ever feel them again. I didn't know if there would be something in my life that would ever be as extreme as my career in sport was; and I was scared of never finding it again, of finding out who I was without it.

I feel all filled up but empty inside
Those porcelain dolls laugh because I'm just as sick as
  them
They've won
Those sunken eyes and smoke-filled lies tease me
Play with me
Save me from their wicked hands
They hold on so tight I can't break free
This doesn't feel right
So many smiling faces and open arms
But my eyes play tricks on me
I don't see what they see
I don't feel what they want me to feel
But I'm kidding myself
I'm just like them
C'mon doll, use me, use me till I shatter
Then everyone will see how broken I really am

True love. My
mother's parents,
Flora and Victor
Poto.

Poolside. Full of life
at age one.

Daddy's little girl.
With my father at
home, aged three.

One of our last
vacations to Florida.
With my mother
and sister, at age
four.

My first year of competing at age
seven (with the boy haircut that was
grown out immediately).

My first taste of glory at age
eight. I was hooked.

Giving it everything I had at my first international competition in Calais, France, aged 11.

Yin and yang. My teammate and best friend in 2002 before everything was about to change.

On the World Cup Circuit as Canadian National Champion in 2004.

With my longtime coach Mimi at the 2003 Corbeis Essonnes Grand Prix in France.

Taking a second to breathe. Grand Prix training session in France, 2005.

Competing at 2002 National Championships as a Senior level gymnast for the first time.

With my teammates after winning Team Gold at the 2006 Commonwealth Games in Melbourne, Australia.

Competing at the 2007 World Championships where I qualified for the Beijing Olympics.

With my father in Patras, Greece after I qualified for the 2008 Olympics at World Championships.

'ith my teammates outside the practice gym before Olympic
alifiers. Sharing one of our last moments together.

(*Above*) My personal cheering section at the 2008 Olympic Games.

(*Above right*) With my coach Mimi at the 2008 Beijing Olympic Games, getting ready for the Opening Ceremonies.

My big sister and I celebrating our time in Beijing at the 2008 Olympics.

Chapter 5:
Rock Bottom

For any young person growing up in today's cluttered, commercialized world, the pressure to be beautiful is all around us. What we really define beauty as has been twisted and contorted to mean something artificial, unattainable, and unhealthy. It fills our minds from the minute we wake in the morning and see our favourite celebrities telling us what yogurt to eat or shampoo to use, to the girls at school or work that starve themselves to squeeze into a size 0. Even on a crowded subway, there are magazines in your face with images of "beauty" plastered all over them, re-shaped and re-coloured to look different, but in the end they're all the same. The obsession with being thin is unfortunately here to stay. No matter how many designers say they won't put deathly skinny models in their runway shows to help young women with their self confidence—it doesn't matter. It has seeped so far into our society and subconscious that I've seen 12-year-olds throwing up after they eat, or calling other girls fat. How I loathe that word "fat". A word that stings even as I say it. A word so small, yet powerful enough to make someone breakdown inside so slowly that they lose who they are. A meaning that can hit someone so hard they will forever feel as though the wind has been knocked out of them when they look in the mirror; a constant reminder that they're not good enough. The very use of the word from other women makes me sick to my stomach, especially when I see girls who are also struggling with coming into their own, bully the unpopular ones: the girls who look different, who are bigger. They use it against each other when competing for a job or a relationship. The judgment that has begun to take over our lives hurts us as women more than we can possibly imagine. We judge a girl before we even know her: "There's the fat girl no one thinks is going to be popular, so why would I want to spend time with her?" Or they think that picking on her is so easy and makes them feel better about themselves. These are statements I've heard from the young women I coach and mentor, girls I passed in the hallways of the high school I worked in, and the business women gossiping at lunch. We use this language and then we laugh as if it's acceptable. No one seems to have a problem with it at all, and the fact that women think it's okay just allows men to do the same. We've all been in a group of people when we've heard a guy describe some girl walking in as fat, and laughing. The response is usually well received at the table with the girls rolling their eyes, but accepting it, and most of the time joining in to make themselves feel more attractive. Does that really make you feel better knowing that you've hurt someone, knowing that they'll cringe a little more when they look at themselves? Knowing that because of what you said or did, they will hide their bodies with layers of clothes and try and become invisible. I would know. I've been there.

My life in gymnastics revolved around what I looked like. Forget the inner beauty pep talk because that didn't matter at all. How thin I should be was the most important question. When I was a little girl playing sports, I had no concept of how skinny I was and if that was a good thing or why that would even matter. I was so completely oblivious to the stress it caused women and the pressure they put on themselves. I believe the longer you stay in this bubble of self-love, the better grounded you are growing up, and the more likely you are to keep a good head on your shoulders when faced with adversity. When you're exposed to people who accept others for who they are, you keep an open mind about embracing people who are different from you, whether it's based on race, religion or appearance. That horrible gut-wrenching feeling you get when someone attacks your racial background is the same as an attack on your appearance. The ability to make someone feel as low as they possibly can is a talent that I never hope to master. I was a tiny little kid, and stayed pretty small throughout my adolescence. I was the shortest in my class, muscular but lean. I wore what I wanted, if it was trendy or not, and didn't think twice about it. Those were the days.

As I got older, I was still the happy tomboy, racing the guys and never being the one they looked at in "that" way. I was fit and an athlete, so the girls didn't judge me either, and was fortunate to never really be bullied or picked on. Sport was my saving grace. It all happened so fast once I turned twelve and propelled into my high performance career. By fifteen I was novice national champion and two-time junior Canadian national champion, racking up international trophies and medals, jetting all around the world, climbing higher and higher. Life was good, and I never expected things to change because I was riding so fast and so high that I was just flying. Then my entire life came crashing down all around me.

I missed qualifying for the 2004 Olympics and tore two ligaments in my left ankle tripping down the front steps of my house, rushing to practice. Not only was I recovering from the biggest disappointment of my life, and trying to put the crushing defeat behind me, but having to sit at home for three months on my couch nursing an ankle that would not cooperate with me, was hell. So instead of being in the gym where I loved to be, and getting my mind off Athens, I was parked on my couch with too much time to think. As a young female athlete, this age is always the trickiest. Your body starts to change, and for gymnasts, this can be career ending. If you grow too much too quickly, it can throw off your balance. And if you spend a season trying to get used to it, you can miss your chance, and before you know it you watch your career fizzle out in the blink of an eye. My problem wasn't my height. I was growing slowly, still all legs, but those three months of "rest" drastically changed my body type. No longer was I this little bodiless girl. Breasts, hips and thighs later, I was the definition of a young women. Not something my coaches were too pleased about.

I cursed my Italian ancestors for giving me this curvy shape, and the worst was that I didn't really notice my body changing until it was too late. I will never forget the look on their faces when I walked back into the gym for the first time. A mixture of disgust, confusion and panic, I think. Just what a self-conscious teenager really needs. From that day on everything changed, and my body became my obsession, my weakness.

To be clear, I was muscular, almost 17 years old at 5'7" and about 130 lb; which is pretty normal. I'm not saying I came back grossly overweight for my age. In fact, the very idea that I was "overweight" was disgusting and hysterical. I can only see it like that now, years later after I've had time to come to as much peace as I can with what was done to me, and what I was made to believe. Unfortunately for my sport, what you look like is just as important as what you do out there on the floor. The typical rhythmic gymnast should be as tall and as skinny as she possibly can be: a deadly stereotype that has driven girls to the hospital. The top girls look more like starved ballerinas than athletes. Even when my weight wasn't an issue, I still never looked like that. I always had muscle and a body type that wasn't accepted but tolerated. Now all of a sudden, after I had the worst year of my life, not only was I not good enough to make it to the Olympics, but now I was too heavy to be competing for Canada.

I had come back to the gym in the fall with a few months to train before my first national competition in front of our whole community. Until then, I loved being among my teammates from coast to coast, showing the judges and coaches just how much I had improved and how much I wanted to be there vying for the top spot. I was at my best when I was at a competition getting ready to do my thing, and I lived to perform. It was my time.

Within two seconds of walking into the gym, all eyes were on me. I could hear the whispers, and feel the once-overs scanning me up and down, in shock at this new Alex. "What happened?" was the question of the week. My coach got attacked by everyone: parents, coaches, judges. The looks of pity, sadness, and just plain confusion were priceless. My confidence plummeted. Hit rock bottom. And then I had to squeeze myself into a skintight suit that left nothing to the imagination, and parade in front of hundreds of people who thought I was fat, and attempt to perform at my best. That small pain inside my chest that day was just the start of a hole that was being created inside me; the beginning of the eventual damage it would all cause, leaving me hollow and empty inside.

After the competition was over, I had won my second national title regardless of being so "overweight". I couldn't even be proud of it as I saw them come right for me: coaches, judges, advisors. All I remember from those "meetings" were certain words: "heavy," "lose weight," "eating habits," etc. I could barely look any of them in the eyes, and I sat there like a stone, head hung so low, biting back tears and only moving slightly to lift my chest and take in small breaths. But I never could hold them back.

I began to look at myself differently from that very first day, and would never see my own beauty through my eyes again. It was gone, not that I didn't try and fight them. From that moment on, the conversation was always about my weight. I saw their eyes on my thighs, my face. It was as if they knew exactly where that pound I gained yesterday went on my body. And if I lost a pound, it didn't matter because if it wasn't 10 lb, then it wasn't worth a comment. I would show up in the gym to train every day, and cringe as I rolled on my thin black tights, tiny shorts and sports bra. Only this time, instead of the snug tank top I used to put on, I began to hide within my clothes, finding baggy t-shirts to throw on instead. I would layer and layer to somehow shrink inside them: thigh-high leg warmers, loose shorts... anything that hugged my curves was thrown under my bed and kept there. My family must have seen what was going on, but what could they do? I was a quiet, moody, private, high performance 16-year-old athlete. I came home at night after training, and the last thing I wanted to do was talk about my weight. My mother saw the inevitable breakdown, and how it got from bad to worse faster than she could have imagined. There were too many triggers and emotional traumas to count, but enough to get me to a point where I hated myself, and where hurting myself seemed the only option.

Those first international competitions with "The New Alex" brought more attention and more pressure for my immediate weight loss. There were no nutritionist consultations, no intelligent, healthy advice—just lose at least 5kg by next week or the next competition. It was as if I was supposed to change dramatically overnight. With straight and absolutely dead serious faces, they would say that if I just ate lettuce and some lean protein, then all our problems would be gone. I wasn't sure if they ever really cared about me as a person, or cared more about what I could do for them. The future of our sport was on my shoulders, it seemed, and I felt the hawks hovering over me. The funny thing was that I would never admit how deeply damaged I was. My friends and family knew I was battling with my body, trying to lose weight and make everyone happy, and they were there for me in the only way they knew how to be. My girlfriends would always watch me to make sure I was eating; and if I wasn't, they would gently confront me about it. And I thank them for that. It must've been so hard to watch me self-destruct, but also be so strong at the same time. I got pretty good at making people think that everything was really "okay, I swear". It became a part of my life, a persona that I took on that hid my dirty little secret. I poured my heart out in journals that I can't even read today, and masked my problem from the world. I would pretend that I didn't care, getting angry instead of hurt in front of my teammates, and using an "I could care less" attitude in public when actually, all I cared about was my body. I became obsessed with mirrors, trying to catch a glimpse of myself in windows, making sure I looked okay, that I was hiding myself, and that everything was perfectly in place. I would spend hours devising outfits to look like I didn't hate my body, when all I did was pick myself apart. I was never happy with what I saw staring back at me. Shopping became a horror where I hated anything I put on and over analyzed the sizes. Nothing was ever good enough, and I couldn't lose weight as fast as I wanted, and didn't understand why it was so hard. I would stand in front of my mirror at home pinching my fat, sucking everything in and imagining what it would be like if I was that thin. I would take pictures of myself and compare them from week to week, getting a sick pleasure out of seeing my body shrink in front of my eyes, only to gain it all back again in a few days. This was my crash diet phase. All I could think of was how to lose weight. It consumed me. All the while, I was training like a maniac and starting university, thrown into a new world of pressures to face. I read every magazine, every article, every piece of advice on speeding up your metabolism, shrinking sizes and dropping weight. I would see my girlfriends around me be able to do it, why couldn't I? It was infuriating to wake up every day and hate myself, never wearing jeans because it showed too much of my body. Long sweaters became my life.

No matter what I did, nothing seemed to work. It got to a point where I became so depressed I would lie awake in bed at night, numb, praying that I would wake up and miraculously everything would be like it used to be, that I would be one of the skinny girls again. Food became a hot topic in my house, with my mother having to make different meals for all of us. I put my family through so much. I would come home from training and one little thing in the kitchen would set me off: Italian bread cut up for my dad and sister, pasta being served, or anything that I couldn't eat. My temper was so short that my mood swings became unbearable in the house. I took all my anger, all of my hurt out on my mother, and she took it graciously and lovingly knowing that she couldn't help me, when that's all she wanted to do. She was always there with open arms. The problem was, I never wanted them. It was weak in my mind, and I couldn't believe that I had let all the pressure get to me. I was stronger than that, I was tougher than that, and I hated who I had become and couldn't face myself, so I could never let anyone in to help me. There were days when I would rifle through the fridge screaming that there was no food, being a selfish, inconsiderate brat, throwing a temper tantrum and storming out of the kitchen, leaving my mother to breakdown—

only to come back hours later when she wasn't around, and eat as much as I could. It made no sense, but I took everything out on her. Some days I would find her at the kitchen table silently crying, and I knew it was me. Her tears slowly ran down her face, hitting the countertop effortlessly. Just being in the kitchen was emotionally draining for me as everything became a forbidden enemy. I would avoid the room as much as I could, hoping to trick my stomach into thinking it didn't need food. When my parents didn't know what else to do with me, they took me to see a nutritionist. This backfired miserably. Not only did she tell me to eat more—but foods I was strictly not allowed: bread, potatoes, carbs. Everything I put in my body was scrutinized and watched by everyone: my teammates, my parents, my coaches, our judges, anyone in the gymnastics world. It was as if it was disapproving to even eat, and I became paranoid. I could see people watching my portion sizes or what I drank. "How many calories were in that Gatorade?" I turned to Splenda and aspartame to get any flavour in anything, and would load it into my plain yogurt, coffee, tea and cereal. Anything to give me flavour and cut calories. Let's see how few calories Alex could eat in one day without passing out. And when I could see what I could do and survive, it only fuelled me to keep going. I was burning a hole in my stomach with my habits, turning to coffee to keep me going through the day. I would wake up and hold out on eating for as long as possible, sometimes drinking eight cups of coffee a day to keep my head up in class and my body moving in training. When I caved, I would try and eat as healthy as possible, finding that I could lose 5 lb in a week this way. I was never happier than when I was losing weight. But I would get to day ten and crash, my stomach twisting, my body completely giving out and holding on to fat for dear life; and I would binge eat on anything I could find. It was disgusting, stuffing my face with literally anything, including whole boxes of cereal or crackers. I would feel so awful afterwards that I could barely contain myself, so disappointed that I could do that to myself. I put my body on this roller coaster for years, yo-yoing up and down, being able to gain or lose 10 lb week to week. The worst part was that my performance suffered, and I was never truly comfortable competing ever again.

In my sport you have to do the World Cup circuit with the other countries' national champions. You had to be out there in front of the judges, consistently putting in solid performances to keep up with everyone else. It was a political nightmare, but had to be done. The more you competed, the better you got and the more chances you had to be seen as one of them, the best in the world. At a competition with only twenty or twenty-five of the best rhythmic gymnasts in the world, I was always the biggest. Even if I lost a few pounds, I was still the fattest. I couldn't compare to the 5'10" 100 lb girls who topped the podium. They would look at me as if I was an outcast, and would snicker and laugh when they saw me. I knew what they were thinking: "Is this fat cow actually any good? What is she doing here?" It ate slowly away at my confidence, and I would warm up and stay in the corner of the practice gym not wanting to be noticed. In a performance sport, you have to want to be noticed, and go out there and show them that. In these early years of battling my weight, I lost that special part of me, that fighter. Every day at the hotel of whatever city we happened to be in that week, Kiev, Paris or Moscow, there would be a special room for everyone at the competition with buffets of food. Anytime I came close to the buffet table, the eyes would be on me. I would scan the room seeing who was in there, how they were related to me and if they knew our coaches or would rat me out. I stuck with lettuce and maybe some meat. There were days when I was so hungry that I would sneak a small piece of bread into the pocket of my Canadian tracksuit jacket, sweating over the anxiety of getting caught. At the end of the year my mother would find stale pieces of crumbled bread in my jackets. Something that once seemed normal is so horrific to me now. I would sew snacks into the lining of my suitcase should anyone ever come to my room unexpected. I became so crafty that I had a whole system down of how I was going to survive. I would starve myself for them; and it took years to admit it, but I did. Not only did I turn to coffee, but gum too. This should have been a dead giveaway to people, but I don't think they wanted to believe it; and if they did know, what were they going to say? I had wanted one thing my entire life, and my weight, one of the worst issues a teenage girl can have, was the only thing standing in my way. I was going to lose that weight in whatever way I could, and my teammates watched me do it. They were the ones that really saw what happened behind those closed hotel doors, our makeshift homes. They saw the real me. Those girls—Yana, Carly, Stef, Ali, Demi...—you got me through it. You held my hand through the lowest part of my life, you let me vent and cry to you, and you gave me your support and love. You wanted my dream to come true as much as I did, and you are all my beautiful sisters.

It was a vicious cycle that I seemed caught in for years. I think back to that scared little girl alone in my head. I was trying to be so strong, and knew that this weight issue was the reality of my sport. I chose this life. No one was forcing me to be there. My parents just wanted me to be happy. Never in my life did they push me to continue, and if anything, there were times when I'm sure they would've welcomed my retirement. Both 2005 and 2006 were rocky years for me where I was nowhere near the shape I should've been in. I couldn't compete, and it was as if my head shut down my body. Negativity coursed through my veins, my self-confidence plummeted, and I dreaded walking off the floor after my event to face "them". At this level, it's not just you and your coach anymore. It's you and all the judges, gymnasts all around the world, your sport's entire organization and the Olympic Committee in Canada—the people who were giving you money because you were supposed to be able to perform. Every mistake you make is observed, analyzed, and thanks to technology, replayed over and over again. Rankings and scores are flashed the second they happen, and broadcast into homes across the globe. Chat rooms and international Web forums scrutinize every gymnast, and I could never get the courage to look. My weight had become an international scandal. Forget that I was one of the best rhythmic gymnasts out there, that didn't matter. The size of my thighs was way more important. At my lowest, I would always be sent away for weeks at a time to compete and train in Europe, with only coaches for company. I remember feeling like I wanted to run away and never look back. The minute I sat down in the front seat of the loaded car, with my mom starting the very familiar drive to the airport, I turned into this miserable, sour thing. I knew exactly what I was walking into, and I didn't know if I was strong enough to get through it. Behind closed doors, thousands of miles from those people who could protect me, I felt hopeless. My life was in other hands—what I did, what I ate, where I slept. It was all carefully planned so that I would be whipped into shape no matter what cost. In some small town in France outside of Paris, or an Eastern European city, I would live day in and day out in my own little dungeon in my head. My coach would push me until I cracked, until I found that fourth wind out of pure anger and spite, wanting to show her that I wasn't weak, that I could do it and wouldn't give up. Those breakthroughs, those hours of pure adrenaline and raw drive to keep my legs moving—they were the best times of my life. The satisfaction of knowing that you could push through was better than any medal.

If I had a different body I may have reached even greater heights, and I truly believe that. My weight brought any success I had a little notch back down, with more pressure mounting up. I dragged it around with me, felt it in my legs, my heart. I would have nightmares of feeling paralyzed, and awake in the middle of the night in cold sweats, imagining myself so heavy that I couldn't move, so big that no one could bear to look at me. It's a horrible feeling to get out of bed in the morning and have to strategically pick out what to wear to hide yourself from people. No matter how I would create an illusion that I was thinner, if my face didn't thin out, then no one would believe it anyways. There are weeks of my life that I've blacked out from my memory, pretended like they never happened. The nights that I sat alone on the edge of the bathtub in my washroom, shaking, and holding a toothbrush in my hand, always just one little step away from sticking it down my throat like so many girls I knew. The thoughts that would run through my mind terrified me. I would run the water to try and drown them out: "How hard could it be? You eat, then throw up and get rid of it as if it never happened. Other girls did it. It wasn't abnormal. It was something to be proud of. The skinnier you got, the more other girls were in awe of you." It was sick. I would overhear girls whining that they couldn't do it, that they had spent hours in the bathroom trying to make their gag reflex kick in, but it just wouldn't work. Their bodies were holding strong. This was a typical dinner conversation for us. You learnt to admire the girls who were deathly skinny, asking yourself why you couldn't look like that. But even worse was figuring out how you were going to look like that against all odds.

Every competition that didn't go well was almost always blamed on my weight. I would be called into hotel rooms and hear that I would be nowhere, no one, if things didn't change. When I would miraculously lose weight, even though I didn't perform well, the performance never mattered. I could do no wrong then, the mistakes weren't as big of a deal. In the mind of a young girl, this pattern became ingrained in my head, and losing weight became the number one obstacle standing in my way. Even the weight I lost didn't make me happy, it was never good enough. There was always more fat to lose, more inches to come off, and a smaller size to fit into. I would hole myself up on the top bunk in a tiny Parisian room, earphones in, and a supply of gum that would soothe the hunger pains, and I would furiously write in my journal until my hand would ache, ignoring the pile of school work I had photocopied and lugged halfway around the world with me. This wasn't real life, I couldn't concentrate on school. Those days, I would wake up in the morning and take the local bus to the gym alone, where I had to workout with a trainer who didn't speak a word of English. He trained French boxers, and I was along for the ride. My lunch break was my only alone time, and I would run across to the little convenience store from the sports complex, so mad, tired and upset, that I would buy individual packages of chocolate cake and eat them as if I hadn't eaten in days. The locals passing me on the street would look at me like I was crazy. I would wolf it down as I walked back to the gym, knowing that I had to finish it or throw it away before I turned the corner and would be in sight of any potential onlookers from the gym. I walked back into the gym with a smirk on my face, thinking I had won some secret battle in my head, and I had tricked them. In the end, it was only putting me further into the ground, burying me deeper until I was so far over my head that nothing seemed real anymore.

I pride myself on never stepping on a scale in front of anyone, despite them desperately trying to get me to do so. I refused to subject myself to that in front of my teammates and everyone who mattered in our sport. I wouldn't let them take my pride from me in that way. They took it in other ways, but I would never offer it up willingly. Today, I can't look at a scale again as it brings back so many horrible memories of wishing and hoping that little screen would flash a lower number, believing that it was lying to me. The very thought of standing on one gives me goose bumps, and I shudder when I have to step onto one for my doctor at my annual checkup. I don't even look, but just let her write it down and be done with it. I'll never define myself with a number ever again. It's just a number, an insignificant few digits that can't say anything about who you are, what you believe in or what you love. It doesn't make you any more or less of a person. You are you, regardless of what the scale says. Don't let it dictate your life. I learned how that "special" little number and the approval of others swayed my mood, my mindset, and my whole persona. The power it held was instrumental in the choices I made and how I perceived myself. I lost friends, potential boyfriends, even the relationship with some of my family members over what this was doing to me. Anything I put into my mouth would start me imagining where it would be going on my body the next day. Another piece of cheese would mean another thirty minutes on the elliptical. Was it worth it? That became my thought process, every minute of every day.

By the start of 2006, things hadn't gotten better. I was still too heavy, and the Commonwealth Games were coming up in Australia. These were my first, big multi-sport Games since the 2003 Pan American Games when I was just an inexperienced gymnast thrown into the spotlight. These Games were important for my country, and I needed to come out guns blazing and take it. During the last Commonwealth Games in Manchester, England, Canada won five gold medals out of the possible six in rhythmic gymnastics, and so I had a reputation to live up to. My whole team knew it. We walked into the selection meet knowing that the judges were keeping in mind who should be heading Down Under, and who would make the top three that weekend. The pressure was on, and I came out on top, but there was something different about me and everyone saw it. I had lost my heart, my fire. I was a robot out there going through the motions because I had to. But that love I had for the sport was missing.

After the meet, we had a two-day camp in Montreal with the team that would be going to Australia. I didn't even participate. We were all warming up that cold February morning when I got pulled into a "meeting". I walked into a room full of people with no one on my side. If I didn't lose weight, I would not be able to compete at the Commonwealth Games. It was unacceptable to look the way I did and represent the country. I now take in that sentence, slowly this time, letting the words sink in. At the time, as an eighteen-year-old girl, I was hysterical, and couldn't even talk. It was one of those full body cries that turn you into a blubbering mess. It was awful. The last year had built up inside of me, and I just let it out. They directed me to Jenny Craig. An elite athlete, a national champion, having to call Jenny Craig to tell them I was fat and needed help. I couldn't train, I couldn't think. I got out of there so fast that my teammates knew exactly what had happened. To see them feel for me so strongly gave me hope that I could get through this.

No one would actually have stopped me from competing in Australia, but they poked and prodded me at every opportunity they could get. I went down there and won six gold medals, breaking a world record for my sport... at my size. That moment meant more to me than anything. What I looked like didn't have to matter, and I wanted to show all those young girls out there that they don't have to fit a mould to be accepted. Never let anyone tell you that you can't do something.

I had accepted that I would never look like those girls I envied, but I would do whatever I could to get in the best shape I possibly could. This newfound plan seemed to work well for me mentally, but not physically. I would train for four hours, then hit the elliptical and treadmill each day for at least an hour and a half, and then go back to the gym to train again. I started working out with the greatest trainer I know, and without him I would have never stayed sane. He was careful to let me do my thing, but he guided me. He was absolutely incredible, and not only was he my trainer, but my psychologist, mentor and friend. It was a breath of fresh air coming to see him every other day during those hard couple of months. He couldn't care less what they told me, and thought that those people telling me I was overweight were crazy. I was strong, powerful and dynamic, and he saw how beautiful that was and asked me if I wanted to be the fastest gymnast out there, the one who could turn heads with her power and strength. I couldn't help but smile. So that's exactly what we did. When I was with him I have never felt more healthy and athletic in my life. He brought me back to life, and I will never be able to thank him for that. When they broke me down he picked me back up, and I would spend hours and hours at the gym with him because it felt like home. After our sessions, he would sit down with me and make sure I ate properly, adding some chicken or protein to my plate, trying to make me understand how important it was to fuel my body with foods that would help me, not hinder my potential. I was at my healthiest with him by my side. You get blinded when you are surrounded with so much negativity that you don't know how to be positive anymore, and you become unable to understand the other side. I could hardly believe there was any other way to look at myself. It didn't matter how many times my parents told me I was beautiful or my sister tried to make me see how incredible I was—nothing worked. I could nod my head and say I understood, but I didn't believe it. Inside I was twisted and torn up, making scrapbooks of models that I wanted to look like, and diaries of my food intake and body measurements. I would have probably kept that measuring tape under my pillow if I thought my mom wouldn't have found it. I was leading this secret life and shutting the rest of the world out, not letting anyone get close to me.

As it got closer to Olympic Qualifiers, the stress I placed on myself was more than I could bear. I was having the best training of my life and hitting personal bests in Europe and all over the world, but the pressure to be thin to make it to the Olympics caught up to me. I could now count down the weeks until I walked into Greece for the World Championships, and it all of a sudden dawned on me that there was no more fooling around with this weight thing. No more just monitoring the situation and making sure I was stable and healthy—I needed to do something drastic. I wasn't quite sure how I was going to do it, but it's scary what you can put your mind to when you feel so strongly about something. So I did the unthinkable.

I starved myself until I could see the pounds melt off, only eating in front of people to make it seem as though everything was okay. The headaches and stomach torture were worth it, I told myself; and the more praise I received for losing weight, the more motivated I became. For the first time in my life, people were looking at me and smiling again, sighing in relief that I had finally cut weight. It was as if they thought I sat at home and stuffed my face with chocolate and pizza, Italian home-cooked meals and anything else I could find, being greedy, inconsiderate and careless, like I didn't care, like I didn't want the Olympics bad enough… like I chose to be fat. I could see it on their faces. I was in complete denial the entire year, training eight hours a day on five hundred calories or less, trying to avoid water to dehydrate myself before I competed. It became so normal that I didn't think anything of it. I loved it. No one dared to say a word, and the next, precious few months could be the end of it all. I know how worried my loved ones were, even my trainer and physiotherapist, and everyone was telling me how thin I had become, but not as a compliment. I didn't care, and what's worse is that I didn't believe them. There were still pounds to lose, and I was still nowhere near being a size 0, which was the ultimate goal. I went from a size 6 to a size 2 in the blink of an eye, too fast to maintain, but I was on a mission. I don't know how I had enough energy for the amount of work I put my body through. I can only think that it was the adrenaline of being so close to the end of the tunnel that carried me. I picked up the worst habits you could think of, like running on Red Bull. And believe me, it does give you wings! Caffeine became my middle name. So dangerous. So stupid. There were days when I would look at myself in the mirror after a hot shower and write in the mirror the words I couldn't say:

"I hate you."

"Help."

"I don't want to die."

The fuzzy silhouette of my face was barely visible as I wiped those words away, those thoughts from my head. "Just a few more weeks," I kept telling myself, "you're so strong, you can do this". I kept packets of honey in my purse for when I felt so faint I needed a shot of sugar to keep me from dropping. Yet it was so easy. I was travelling all over the world on my own, never under supervision, never accountable to anyone or anything besides showing up in the gym and doing my job. As long as I did that and competed well, no one asked questions. I was a young woman who should have known better, but the years of emotional abuse had warped my own morality. When I walked into World Championships, the thinnest I had ever been, I gave it my all, and everyone noticed. It couldn't have been more perfect, and I had the best competition of my life. When I qualified for the Beijing Olympic Games, I came back to life, woke up from the nightmare I was living, and opened my big eyes.

What I looked like didn't matter anymore. I was free. I have never felt so alive, and gave in to all my senses. I stayed up all night celebrating with my family and teammates who had come to Greece to watch me. I ate and drank in excess, toasting the year and the place I had come from. I met my best friend the next week and had ten days on the beach in Greece to enjoy myself and relax. I came home a new woman, and was done with feeling vulnerable and scared, and needed to concentrate on me and only me: my health, my body, my mind and soul. I needed to come to terms with what I did to myself, and to start healing, and lean on my family. It was easier to run away and disappear for weeks at a time when I was struggling than to drag them into it. I know now that I can't do everything on my own, and for those of you who stuck around long enough for me to realize that, you will be in my heart forever.

2008 was a year of learning and growth. I gained back most of my weight and almost had a career-ending injury mere months before the Olympics. The injury became my main focus, and my weight was a distant second for once. I cared more about being able to walk than what I looked like in my bathing suit, and it was eye opening for me. After I got to the Games with my ankles taped up so tightly that they were being held together, I knew that what I had overcome to get there meant more to me than what I looked like. I slid into those competitive suits one last time, and walked out there with no body image issues, no regrets, no looking back.

Chapter 6:
There's Always a Reason to Smile

etiring at twenty-one was always the plan, but I knew going from working out for a living to a normal university student would have a huge change on my body. I wasn't exactly ready for it, but I knew that I had to handle it as best as I could and stay healthy. Yes, I lost muscle. Yes, I gained weight. Yes, I wasn't happy about it. No, I didn't waste my time and energy worrying about it anymore. I had big plans to stop training and stay really active. I was a sports girl who loved to be out there running around in the summer and hitting the gym. I figured I would never lose that drive to be fit and active. After seventeen years in the gym, I gave myself a vacation and stepped away from the daily, disciplined regimen I was used to, and gave my body a rest. A few months of lapping up as many sleep ins and big meals as I could, especially those home-cooked meals from my mom, and I was ready to get back into shape. I wasn't fully healed up, I had knee and ankle problems still, but when I put my mind to something, I do it, and I stick by it. I have always tested my limits, and I carefully pushed my ankles every day, getting stronger and doing a little bit more in the gym.

January rolled around and a few girlfriends and I headed up north to a cabin for my birthday. To be clear, I snowboard, not extremely well, but I definitely don't ski. This was me convincing myself that I was coordinated enough to ski. It would be embarrassing if I couldn't, so I thought I'd just go and have fun with my friends. I couldn't have been more wrong.

The weekend turned into a disaster that would throw me right back into my dark little world that took over a year to climb out of. Everyone thought that if I knew the basics I could probably ski down a blue hill (like I knew what that meant), and be fine. First off, I fell off the chairlift. With my ego bruised and confidence shaky, I shook it off and thought, "How much worse could it be now?" Throughout the course of the day, I fell over thirty times, broke two ski poles, body checked my friend twice (who was just trying to help me), cracked my ski mask, and became officially known as the girl who couldn't get off the chairlift. It was the most frustrating day of my life, probably the most embarrassing as well, but I really wanted to get it right and kept going until I got down that run without falling. Hours later, I finally did it, and I've never felt like I've accomplished a bigger feat. Funny for an Olympian to say that, but it's true. So I was skiing! There we all stood, exhausted and snow happy, wondering if we should do one last run. Here is where I wish I could reverse time and never let myself get on that ski lift. But there was no stopping me, I was pumped. It all happened so fast I hardly remember now. I was on the same run that I had been practicing on all afternoon, but with a little more confidence, which is always dangerous for me. I pointed my skis downward and took off, racing by everyone else, addicted to the speed. I could feel the wind on my face; see the blur of the trees beside me. I couldn't wipe the smile from my face, and felt invincible. I made a big turn, sweeping across the mountain, only to realize in a split second that I was losing control. I knew it was coming, the epic fall, but I was going to try and save myself as best I could. Tilting my skis upward, I tried to slow down only to catch an edge and go flying. It probably looked as though five people had collided and rolled down the hill. Snow flew up so high it seemed to touch the skis dangling from the chairlift passing by. My right ski didn't pop off, and as my body went hurdling down the hill, this ski got stuck in the snow and ripped my knee apart. I heard that snap, and my heart dropped. There was silence as my body hit the hard ice and slid down the steepest part of the hill. I came to a stop halfway up the hill with my left leg crushing my right. At first, I didn't feel anything, just the pounding of my heart. And then it hit me. The pain was unbearable. My whole body was on fire, and I started to panic. I screamed but nothing came out. I was dead silent. My friend threw off her skis and climbed up the hill to get to me, and I've never been more relieved to see her face. All I could tell her, repeatedly, was to get my left leg off my knee. The weight of it on my mangled knee was more than I could handle. She must've been so scared. A couple had seen what had happened and called ski patrol, putting up their skis in an "X" behind me, which apparently is all protocol, but I had absolutely no idea what was going on. They were trying to make me laugh, I remember that, but all I could feel was sick. In that moment I didn't know what I had just done, but I couldn't move. Within minutes, the snowmobile pulled up, and they tried to calmly explain to me how they had to get me down the hill in a body bag. I didn't care that I was going to be shuttled down in a zipped-up bag like a dead body, but the very thought of moving was terrifying. I kept my eyes shut and tensed up all the muscles in my body as they lifted me up and put me on the stretcher. "Don't throw up, just please don't throw up," I said to myself. That ride down the hill was horrible, painful and mortifying. Six teenage boys who were working up there for the weekend had to carry me into the medical hub. I covered my face with my hands as they put me down so the medic could check me out. I could have killed this woman because she decided to lift up my leg and shake off my ski boot. I almost passed out, and the colour drained from my face as my girlfriend started yelling at the woman. I have never been more proud of her. They put a splint on my leg and had to get me to the hospital immediately, but I had gone into shock by this time, shaking and numb. The pain spread from my leg to my back. An ambulance would have been a few hundred dollars that I didn't have, so these scrawny boys carried me outside and had to maneouvre me into the backseat of my friend's little two-door car. This scene should have been caught on camera. We had no idea how the hell I was getting out of that car, but I was in, and we were on our way to the hospital. I was praying that

I had either broken my knee or strained some ligaments. I didn't want to hear those three letters come out of anyone's mouth, even though we were all thinking it—ACL: anterior cruciate ligament.

The paramedics didn't know how to pull me out of the backseat without me causing them physical harm, but we managed, and before I knew it I was in a wheelchair waiting my turn in the ER. My friends pleaded with the nurses to give me some medication as the pain was getting too much for me to handle, and I could feel it in every single bone in my body. No can do. So we waited and waited in this tiny hospital surrounded by so many sick and bleeding people that my stomach was turning. Any minute I was going to lose my lunch, and then they called my name. After loads of tests, they figured it was just a minor MCL tear (medial collateral ligament), no ACL damage. I would be fine with just ice and no crutches. I could breathe again, with some tears of joy. I went to get off the stretcher and go tell my friends, when I stepped onto my right leg, and with a little bit of pressure, my whole knee collapsed inwards and I face planted on the hospital floor. The day could only have gotten worse if I had smashed up my face somehow; but thankfully someone didn't want me to have the worst day of my life. Turns out that it was much more than just a minor MCL tear. When I got home I went straight to my sports doctor, and he spoke those dreaded letters I never wanted to hear: "ACL". The ligament that can't heal itself once it's torn. The ligament that ends careers. When I do something, I do it full-out, moving from one extreme to the other. If I injure myself, it's never just minor. I take out my whole knee.

I never thought that I could hit rock bottom again. I sat in that room with my doctor—the man who had saved my career the year before by making sure I could compete on my ankles in the Olympics—and I braced myself for the news. With a smile he said, "What did you do, kid? We'll get through this, don't worry". That day I got an MRI and was linked up with one of the best surgeons in Toronto. Surgery was the only option in my mind, and the chance that I wouldn't be able to run again or play sports competitively would bring my life to a standstill. There was still so much I wanted to do in my life. I wanted to dance professionally, perform, compete, and continue to be that risk taker I always was. This injury forced me to rethink who I was and how I was going to live my life with something permanent. I was back on my couch all over again, trying to get the swelling down before I could have surgery. Working out and doing anything active was out of the question as I could barely walk with my crutches. I was miserable and depressed, and went from being in Olympic shape to nothing, with no buffer in between. It was humbling, and the worst part of it was seeing the pity in everyone's eyes. Nothing they could say could make me feel better about myself as I was on crutches in the winter on university campus, living back with my parents, because I couldn't take care of myself, and slowly starting to gain weight again. I was finally back to normal, still pre-surgery, with my range of motion coming back, and being able to walk again, although I couldn't go upstairs or leave my house in case I slipped on the ice or stepped awkwardly off the curb. My biggest fear was hurting myself again, and I hadn't even had surgery yet. My surgeon warned me not to get too comfortable in this state because I was about to go back to zero again. All the work I did to get my strength and flexibility back was going to disappear, and I would have to learn how to walk again after surgery. I nodded, and understood the words coming out of his mouth, but didn't quite expect my recovery to be exactly like what he said. I figured I was strong, stubborn and motivated, and I wouldn't be like one of those people who let pain slow down their progress. We had a very intense recovery plan because I wanted to be back in the gym in the fall, which left six months for recovery. I was ambitious alright, but I was ready to get this over with and get back on my feet.

After surgery, I had apparently woken up earlier than I was supposed to, and they pumped me with some sort of drug until my nerves subsided, and eventually wheeled me in to see my mom. I still hadn't seen my knee as it was all bandaged and wrapped up in a big splint. They taught me how to walk with crutches, and sent me on my way. I went to bed at home that night thinking it really was going to be okay, and smiled knowing I was going to see my physiotherapist tomorrow. Sitting on her table the following day, as she unwrapped my bandages and showed me my scars, was an out-of-body experience for me. Not being able to lift my leg meant I had lost more than 80 percent of my muscle. Looking at my leg and willing it to move, just an inch, was excruciating, and I broke out in a sweat trying to lift it. But it was lifeless. It just lay there, like it had given up. I felt hopeless. Thankfully, everyone put up with my venting and negativity initially, until the tough love set in. My recovery was longer than I would have liked it to be. I had complications, my body rejected my stitches, and I got an infection and had tendinitis from pushing it too hard too fast, of course. But I made it through, I survived the storm. The moral of this story is that you're constantly being tested every single day of your life, and how you choose to handle it determines who you're going to become in the future, and where you're going to go. It was a rocky year, and my weight fluctuated up and down with it, falling back into that familiar pattern of crash dieting and working out. It was hard to want to be able to move when you couldn't, to want to be active and healthy yet stuck in a life that you didn't choose. Accepting the fact that I was out of shape was one of the hardest realizations, but once you can get past it and look to the future, plan your next steps to get healthy and back on track—you can stay positive.

It took over a year and a half, but I recovered. I found myself in a new head space, one where I was proud of my muscles and my body. When I speak to young women and mentor younger athletes, I see what they are battling and the pressures that are coming down on them from all angles. I share my story with them to help them see that it doesn't have to be that way for them. We all need to see the beauty in ourselves, the strength and power we have. There are so many things in life we can't control, but you have to make the best of every situation. See the good even in the worst of times. If you let people get to you, you've let them win and affect your life, and change who you are. Never let others make you feel like less than your worth. Everyone, no matter what shape, size or skin colour, has something inside of them that can bring so much to this world. We need to open our eyes and see that, accept people for who they really are and not who they are trying to be. Take a look at your friends, the people you keep close to you. Make sure they are the ones that no matter what happens will hold your hand, won't be ashamed or embarrassed to be with you, and won't make you feel stupid. You can eat whatever you want in front of them and not feel guilty. The people who really love you, they are harder to find than you think. After years of never feeling good enough, I still fight with this impulse to think the worst of myself. But every day I wake up in the morning, look at myself in the mirror, and I say one thing that I'm thankful for, take a deep breath, get ready for work and smile. There is always a reason to smile. You just have to find it.

I think of you dad when I need strength
Mom, your heart, your incredible heart
How do you do it?
Are you proud of me? Of who I've become?
You pull me in, and arms open wide that will
*   never let go*
Why do you want me?
I am nothing like what you are
My body inked forever with reminders of you
Keep pushing, keep making myself better
Smile for me
Tell me you love me even though I never want to
*   hear it*
Tell me I'll find a love like yours
You're my first, my last, my everything

Chapter 7:
An Orlando Woman

"Identity" is one of those words that creep up on you, with a power behind it that's so purposeful and strong, and with the strength to instill hatred that can last for generations, cause wars, and draw a line between cultures forever. Your identity is who you are and what you believe in that distinguishes you from others. Easy enough. But when you stop and think about it, how many times in your life have you gone against who you are? Followed the crowd or fallen into a pattern that was self-destructive? We've all been there. We've all had those moments of peer pressure whether it's on the field during recess or in the boardroom. Pressure to conform, pressure to be something we're not pervades our lives. You may not see it, but it's there.

Really think about who you are. Why do you do things the way you do? We all know who we are: our name, the city we live in, the job we do. But what you do, where you live and what you're called, doesn't define you. It's how you live your life that defines you. As I look back on mine, I've stayed true to who I am even in my darkest world despite moments of weakness and periods of angst and rebellion—those times where you succumb to outside pressure and give in. I knew what I was doing to my health, and I made the sacrifice, but I never lost sight of reality, which is why I could heal myself.

I'm still stubborn, headstrong, a workaholic and a perfectionist who wants it all. It's a pretty terrifying combination, but there's no way I would have ever achieved what I have at my age without working as hard, sacrificing as much, and pushing myself like I did.

For a long time I used to think my stubbornness was a bad thing, making life more difficult than it had to be, and something that made me less attractive, less friendly, and a lesser person. Forgetting about what other people think, what's supposedly acceptable, and what you think you want to be—take a good look at who you are, and who you've become.

I've seen people change who they are for others, for a job, and for a glimpse into a new life. A friend of mine once said he was scared of becoming an "empty suit". That has much more meaning than the words can actually express. What really stuck with me was how he said "empty" as if he would become invisible one day, eaten up by this crazy world we live in. But I never believed that would happen to him because we always have a choice, a say in what direction our life is going in, and what we let ourselves get absorbed into. You'll never become an empty suit unless you let it happen. Life is too short to do something that doesn't make you happy. If you struggle with maintaining relationships that used to fill your life with so much energy and warmth, you have to make a change. There are sacrifices that we all make for what we want, and it may not bring you happiness every day, but if the end goal and that long term vision is where you want to be that will make it all worthwhile—so be it. If you believe in what you do and stand behind it, put your head down, work hard and get through it—you can move mountains.

When I look at my life and my career as a Canadian athlete, there were moments where I was scared of what I would become, of what the criticism and of pushing myself to my limits would do to my mind, body, and soul. People have an odd depiction of what a high performance athlete is. They know it's hard, they know we train long hours that seem impossible to the normal person, and fly all over the world competing under immense pressure. And they think we all enjoy every second of it. Personally, there were days where I wanted to walk out of the gym and never look back. Jump on a plane leaving it all behind, and escape to a place where no one knew my name and I could eat and drink whatever I wanted.

There were weeks when emotions got in the way, when fears and insecurities crept in. Athletes aren't these super fit machines that defy all odds and do no wrong. We are human. I once went to a school to speak to students during one of their assemblies, and a small boy looked up at me with this confused look on his face, and said, "You're an Olympian?" There was a little disbelief, because to them I don't look like an Olympian. I'm 5'7" with an average build, pretty strong but not Superwoman. Apparently, I didn't quite measure up to this 12-year-old, and I'm assuming he was expecting some superhero woman to walk through the door that morning. But athletes and Olympians were their age once, dreaming of playing sports for a living and maybe competing for their country. It took us years to get there, and a dedication and drive that we found inside ourselves. Athletes fail just as much as they triumph; even more so in some cases. What sets us apart from others, what makes Olympians so special, is that we have this incredible ability to never give up. No matter what life gives us, we push back and fight. We don't accept anything less of ourselves than our best, and we'll do everything we can to get there. Anyone can do it if you have it inside of you to forget the pain, the pressure and the constant critique. But more than that, if you're not afraid of failing, you can do anything you put your mind to.

So when I think of my identity, sport made me who I am; but it doesn't define me. For many years I was Alex the Gymnast, and I hated it. I was more than that. Gymnastics was what I did, and I loved it, but it wasn't who I was. It was a part of my life that took up a lot of my time and energy. But the person behind it all was just me. Those people who stuck by me throughout all the years I struggled, they know me the best, and will tell you how much I am like my father. My strength, courage, and never-ending love for my family and those closest around me, come from him.

Let me tell you a little something about my father. Paul Victor Orlando, a Sicilian born and raised in Queens, New York, is the life of the party, the office, the gym, the restaurant, the airport... you name it. He's a hit. Wherever he goes, he is a magnet attracting people of all ages and backgrounds, drawing them in with his blunt, ridiculous humour, booming New York accent and party-boy mentality. Anyone who comes in contact with my dad remembers him and his dance moves; and they usually have some story to tell from it. Unforgettable in the best kind of way, my dad is the comedic relief when we need it, and the strong man that protects and cares for his family.

This is the Paul everyone knows. This is the Paul that gets up and shows the young men in the house how to throw a punch or fight like the "old days". He's the guy that out-drinks the teenagers who come into his kitchen. They stare at him a little in awe and a little terrified, but expecting nothing but a good time. It's that brash New York accent, drink in his hand and no bullshit mentality that is so damn endearing.

My dad and I have this unspoken bond that I've come to cherish. It's not something that we need to gush about or draw attention to, but it's there. I can't quite explain it, but it's a connection that doesn't need a lot of talking. The impression my dad has made on me has shaped my life decisions. As I get older, the relationship I have with him grows stronger, and now no longer a little girl or even a young woman, I've become a strong Orlando woman, and not someone to mess with. All those years of him teaching us how to be tough, gave me the confidence to stand up for what I wanted, and go after it. He's the tough, invincible, extremely hardworking father figure who protects and cares for us. He fits that mould perfectly, and I know how fortunate I am to have such a man in my life.

When you think of your parents and where they came from, it resonates with you. It sits in your heart. My father grew up in a tough neighbourhood in Queens. From the stories of ridiculous escapades in his youth, I've pieced together just how rough you'd have to be to survive in that neighborhood. But you'd never hear him complaining. He makes light of his hardships, laughs at the day he got his face bashed in with a baseball bat, and revels in the fact that he was Mr. Tough Guy. He rarely speaks of his younger brother Gasper, the uncle I never got to meet. But when he does, it's always of protecting him, getting him out of trouble or helping him escape the wrath of their father. My grandpa Victor was an absolutely effervescent man. Apparently I'm a lot like him, so it's said. A wise man, intelligent and beautifully articulate, Victor spent all his time providing for his family, but could never find the time to really be there for my father, or go watch him play baseball. He loved his kids with all his heart, and in those times as a new immigrant to America from Italy, he did what he could to give them a better life. One of my favourite photos of my grandpa is of him out on the street in New York holding my father on the palm of his hand, up over his head as if it was nothing. That old black and white photo is yellowing from the outside in, but it's beautiful. The smile that he had drew me in, and I'm told that he was joyful, with a laugh that echoed through the house. He absolutely loved my mother.

Long before my mom came into the picture, my father went through tragedies that changed him forever; a dark, traumatic series of events that my sister and I never knew about. He was just a boy when my grandmother died of a brain tumour, leaving my grandpa Victor to raise two boys on his own. These were not your regular clean-cut all-American boys either. The pressures they must have faced in their neighbourhood each day would break almost anyone now. My grandmother was in her early forties, and beautiful. I look at pictures and see my sister in her: such a strong face, proud but gentle. That kind of loss I can't even imagine. I have friends who have lost parents, and I've sat at the funerals in tears as I watch them struggle with their grieving, with the idea of never seeing their parents again.

My dad was a brilliant young man with a good head on his shoulders, bound for a career in engineering. Then it all changed. There's a big part of my father's life that we never spoke about. A time that we now only learn about in history books and debate over the issues of bad politics, an unfortunate war, and the effects on the countries involved. My father was in the Special Forces Unit of the U.S. Armed Forces, and served two tours in Vietnam when he was just twenty-one years old. His younger brother Gasper was drafted, and proudly followed his big brother to East Asia.

Gasper died two days before he was due to come home, two days before he would have survived the Vietnam War. My father, having already served his time for his country, was waiting in New York with his father, counting the seconds before Gasper was back home. But he never came back. I grew up never knowing anything about Gasper, this handsome young man with big eyes that I've only seen in a picture. He was just a baby when he died, barely a man, with a machine gun in his hands, knee-deep in mud in the jungles of Vietnam. He was awarded the Purple Heart medal of honour, the Bronze Star for valour under fire, and other awards for fighting so bravely for his country. But what does that really matter? Does that make it easier for his family to know that he died gallantly? There's a box hidden in the basement of our house with the American flag folded from his military funeral—a day that is never spoken of, and never will be. Both my father's and my uncle's medals adorn the faded blue and white stars, and I run my fingers over them every now and then when I want to reconnect with the history of my family. We don't ever pull it out. It sits in its dusty, clear plastic box on the highest shelf of our messy basement. No one would notice it there. The look in my father's eyes when he speaks of Gasper is vivid, piercing. The loud, boisterous guy we all know and love disappears, and he gets quiet, uncomfortable. His eyes drop to the floor as if the memories are so repressed that he's trying to hold them down, inside of him. I look at my sister and I could never imagine losing her. The thought is so inconceivable that it makes my stomach turn.

One quiet night when my mom had already gone to bed, I sat at the kitchen table with my dad. The kitchen is a room that has housed the best parties and memories of our lives. It embodies my family. It's the meeting spot, our core. I curled my legs underneath me, leant forward with my elbows on the table, and really talked to my dad. For the next hour we sat at the table and spoke words that had been unspoken for so long. I choked back tears as he told me stories of the horrors that he faced. Children with machine guns—your friends, your brothers—the only men who knew what you were going through, blown to pieces beside you, their blood on your hands and face. The fear of dying every second of your life, and the anguish of forcing yourself to pick up that gun and do what you had to do to survive. I shut my eyes and the tears streamed down my face. There's no way my father lived through that, but now I see that pain in his eyes, those scars he keeps close to his heart. As the words spilled out of his mouth, he was quiet, reflective and pained. The mindset of being able to kill, to be trained to kill, is something so foreign to me, and I would never want to know what that feels like. I placed my hand on his back, and like two statues at the table, we stayed like that for what felt like forever. He shook his dropped head and sighed. He told me what it was like to come back to your country, to your home, where they spat on you and threw rocks at you. Vietnam vets were blacklisted by the community, disrespected. Thousands of young men that fought in the jungles and survived guerilla warfare were ridiculed, shamed. It was disgusting. As much as I don't believe in pointless wars that could have prevented thousands of deaths, the respect I have for those that serve their country is endless. As a proud American teenager, serving your country was an honour. My father, and the thousands of others that survived, had nothing to do with the politics of that war, nothing to do with the decisions that were made at such a high level that kept them in Asia, in the line of fire. The trauma they would have endured over years of combat was horrible enough, but to come home to the country you risked your life for and have everyone turn against you—I shudder thinking about it. Everything that came home with him was thrown out, and there's hardly any evidence that he was even there. A camouflage shirt here or there, a jacket found in the bottom of some dusty old trunk in the basement. But that's really it. There was no reason to hold onto the memories, when all he wanted to do was forget them.

I watched him rehash a past that had been pushed so far down into the deepest corners of his mind. He grasped my hands, stared into my eyes, trying to get me to understand, willing me to see what he saw, to walk in his shoes for a day. I've never felt so connected with him, so a part of who he was. I see it now.

There's always a moment around the holidays when things get serious, when the conversation turns from hysterical laughter to how grateful we are to have each other in our lives. It was my father's turn to talk this time, and for the first time he spoke of his father's heartbreak over losing a wife, a mother, and then his youngest son. My grandpa Victor, always so full of life, was never the same. When the telegram came notifying them of Gasper's death on the battlefield, things changed forever. As emotional as my dad has ever gotten, he told us he has a cross to bear with the death of his brother. He was supposed to protect him, he was supposed to make sure nothing ever happened to him, and he didn't. He wasn't even there when it happened. Thousands of miles away in a war that no one will ever understand, his brother nicked the edge of a land mine with his heel, and lay in a hospital alone until he died, at 21 years old. Such a waste of a life. A life that had so much potential if he had gotten the chance. You can see it in my father's eyes how he feels responsible; and even forty years later, that weight on his shoulders is still there. We try to tell him that there's nothing he could have done, even if he was there beside him. But why Gasper? That's a question that no one can answer. You have to believe in your heart that everything happens for a reason, and that it was his time, even though he was so young. People come in and out of our lives, but they always stay in our hearts, and my dad's brother is there with him, every day.

My sister and I were cleaning up the basement and found a letter from Gasper, his last letter from Vietnam, written two days before he was gone. Two days before he was coming home.

We stood there paralyzed. I wiped the tears off her face before they dripped onto the letter that was shaking in her trembling hands. I put my arms around her and never wanted to let her go.

Losing a sister was something neither of us wanted to speak of, but we were both thinking it. I will never take her for granted again. All the stupid fights, little things that annoy us or just letting ourselves fall out of touch seemed so ridiculously selfish. Life is too short to not appreciate the people we love the most in our lives. It's not worth it. Every time I speak to her or see her I soak it in, and hold on to those memories because you never know when you won't have the chance to anymore.

If you knew my father, you would know what strength is. You wouldn't see a broken man, a man that has carried horrific memories for years, a man that has been surrounded with death and tragedy. You would see who we all see. I finally understand why he is the way he is. I finally understand why I am the way I am. He would do anything for his family. My father would sacrifice anything and everything to make us happy. He would give his life for us, to protect us. But he's firm and strict, and taught us very early on that you have to be strong and not let people walk all over you. You need to own up to your mistakes and keep your head up. You need to push yourself to get the best out of yourself. "Mind over matter, baby," he would say, teasing me. "Pain is nothing, it's temporary. Life is for living, so live it. Take chances, take risks, but be smart. Be grateful for the things you have and how you got them. Give as much love as you possibly can to your family, and never let them go."

Behind his smooth talking, life of the party, hilarious persona, my dad has worked harder than anyone I know. When I feel like giving up and shutting down, I think of him, I channel his energy. I wonder if my dad would even have thought of letting go. There's no way. Whether it's a long day at work where I want to check out and procrastinate, or a workout that I want to give up on—I think of him. Faster, higher, stronger. We can get through anything.

When his father died years later, his own family tried to take everything from him. To see your own blood turn against you like that is inconceivable to me because my family is my rock. They are the only people in this world that I would trust to have my back no matter what I did. I would sacrifice it all for them and can't think of a situation that would make us turn against each other. We don't like each other every day, but the love that's there between us, it's malleable, forgiving, unbreakable. Who I am as a woman has been shaped by this love, by this unbelievable family. I see that my strength, my desire to never stop testing my limits, my resiliency and stubbornness to go after what I want no matter the cost, comes from my father. Thank you Dad for showing me how not to be afraid of who I am, but to embrace it, to embody the independence, the character, and the defiant will that courses through my veins. And I know that not everyone is going to like it, but I'm okay with that.

Chapter 8:
The Girl I Always Wanted to Be

've looked up to my sister Victoria since I was old enough to know that she was special. Before I could even talk, I was fascinated with this beautiful thing in front of me. She played with me, held my fingers in hers, kissed my forehead. But she was different from all those other people around me. She was my protector, my guardian angel.

For as long as I can remember, I've wanted to be her. Four years and a week apart exactly, Victoria Ann (always upset she wasn't like Anne with an "e" of Green Gables) was the most incredible girl I knew. I analyzed her with my big, wide eyes; touched what she touched, ate what she ate. I wanted everything that she had and didn't think that was wrong. I just wanted to be near her, and I drove her insane. My mom let me play with her things when she was at school, when I was little enough to be distracted by Barbie dolls for hours on end. Her room was my dream world: a forbidden forest filled with pixie dust and imaginary creatures. I created a fantasy that came to life in front of my eyes, taking things and hiding them only to forget where I put them afterwards. My mother knew she was in for screams when my sister came home from school, but that was a risk she was always willing to take.

My sister wasn't like me growing up. She loved being the only child, adored by all, pampered and spoiled. I came into the picture and ruined it all. I was there to disrupt her life and throw off the perfect balance she was so used to. She really couldn't stand me, but all I wanted was her love. I was "It," as in "It" is touching my things, "It" is in my way, "It" is bothering me and my friends. I was a brat. I still am. But she is my sister, and the bond between siblings is so strong that it's unbreakable. When I look into her eyes, I know she sees the real me. She can sense my pain, my fear, my happiness. I can't lie to her, and nothing gets past her, even when I try.

Everything I do, everything that I work towards, I know I have her with me. When I grew out of the cute, quiet stage, I was the most energetic, attention-seeking kid you've ever met. Home videos of car rides back from the States or a friend's cottage would consist of my sister sitting in her seat, arms crossed, huffing and puffing. I was out of my chair, jumping in front of her to get on camera, high-pitch whining about when we were going to get home. I wouldn't stop, even when I was being yelled at. I threw my head back and let out a belly laugh. Even as we got older, the age difference was just enough to keep us apart. I was twelve and she was sixteen. Victoria was hot stuff: tall, legs for days, with a body to die for. The boys trailed after her like puppy dogs. She knew it, and she worked it. Hers was a beauty hidden behind dark makeup and strands of hair that would hang in front of her face. I was so envious, so jealous of her life. I hadn't come into any sort of looks, and I was still in that awkward stage, sporty, not quite a young lady, but not a girl anymore. Thankfully, I had gymnastics to distract me from all the superficial, junior high peer pressure. But I longed to be popular like her. I would come home from training late in the evening, and she'd be in her room with a girlfriend whispering about boys and gossip.

As we grew up, she not only saw me transform, but I watched her turn from a quiet student to an outgoing actress, to rebellious skater chick, to singer, university graduate, and then to a beautiful, grown-up kindergarten teacher and soon-to-be wife.

At every stage in her life I was there, staring in awe at her ability to bring laughter all around her and carry herself and her incredible talent with such humility. I like to think I've learned that from her. You would never know that her singing voice could bring you to tears. It rocks you to your very core, fuels your body with movement. I can sit and listen to her for hours, for days. She doesn't see how special she is. I want to shake her sometimes and tell her to use it, use her beautiful talent to inspire, to create, to shape the world around her, because she can. There are people in this world that are given a gift, and they should not turn their back on it. Victoria is one of those people that has it, but for some reason doesn't show it to the world like she should. I would hate to think that's because of me and the sacrifices we made for my dream. No one asked her what her dream was.

There is a piece of me that will always feel that for every good thing that came out of my athletic career, there were a hundred bad things. When I started gymnastics and began to compete, my family never thought in their wildest imagination that I would be training six days a week and flying to Europe and Asia at twelve years old to represent my country. It all happened so fast. My sister knew how much I loved rhythmic gymnastics from the very first day I tried it. She was actually the one that started classes first, and I followed behind her, of course, like with figure skating lessons and ballet. She was my idol. Even though she liked it, she didn't love it. I loved it. I was so competitive, all I wanted to be was the best; and in my recreational classes, I was the best. I could handle the apparatus better, follow the music effortlessly, and win the toe-pointing competition every week. I was the most flexible, and worked on it at home when I didn't have to. It was challenging, different. When my sister gave it up, I stuck with it. For once, this was mine, something that I did for me. My sudden success changed everything, changed the whole dynamic of my family. My career took over.

Victoria was at a performing arts high school, fine tuning her voice. She sang in a chamber choir that won prestigious awards across the board, and spent high school surrounded by some of the most artistic people I've ever met. But that wasn't the focus, and we all knew it. I was the focus. Making sure I got to training on time and spent enough hours with my coach at night; making sure I had a separate dinner prepared for when I got home from practice; keeping on my back about homework and preparing for upcoming trips—this was the focus. Our dinner table conversations were invaded with talk of toe shoes, my coach, my next trip, my teammates. My father and sister kept quiet. It was too much. My mom became my manager, devoting her days and nights to my career, fundraising for my club, and running competitions. It became both of our lives. I would never say that they weren't all supportive of me because they were. My sister has been and always will be my biggest fan, and my father is so proud of me you'd swear he was my agent. But it consumes you. The Olympics were only a few years away, and I had a shot, a real shot. When we realized that, when we truly believed that it could happen, no one was going to stand in my way—even if we all had to change because of it.

My parents tried to split their time and attention equally between my sister and I, and I commend them for that. They were never those parents that were oblivious to the competitive nature of siblings and the affect that my career could have on Victoria. They were aware. I didn't see it until later, but there were so many things that were out of their control. There were gymnastics competitions my mom had to travel to with me, missing my sister's singing performances and big nights. Victoria always had to get a ride with another family, or do something after school. The car was occupied. I was going to training, the airport, or a press conference. The phone never stopped ringing. Day in and day out, my mother was on the phone with other parents, and there were the numerous committees she sat on with our local club or with my coach. Everything went through her—booking flights, confirming competitions—she made sure it was all taken care of. It was a job, but it didn't end at five o'clock. It was 24 hours a day, 7 days a week. The phone could ring at any time, the emails wouldn't stop; and to keep me sane I had to be left out of it. I was young and didn't understand how involved my mom had to be. My job was to show up at the gym and work, keep healthy, be smart about my food and my body, and get enough sleep. These were the things that I was supposed to be able to do easily. But they never were. The stress of being national champion so young was affecting my whole family. All I cared about was my sport and being the best. It was one thing to be chasing the top of the podium, but another to grab that spot and stay there. The pressure on my coach to groom the next Canadian Olympic hopeful began to invade our lives, and my sister rarely saw me those days. Besides the quiet early morning breakfasts we ate together in the kitchen, we both went off to separate schools, and I went directly to training afterwards. When I got home she was already done eating and was in her room or with friends. We didn't even talk. It was a period of time when we weren't really friends. I didn't know anything about her. She was dragged to competitions and holiday shows, but I never went to anything of hers. I was too busy putting training ahead of everything in my life, even my sister.

I'm ashamed to admit it, embarrassed to tell it to the world, horrified that I let it happen, but it's true. I tried to be there, but we fell further apart. It wasn't until she went away to university that we learned to appreciate each other, miss one another. She would make fun and tease me, but it didn't matter because any time she gave me attention I was glowing. Some of the best memories I have with her are when we were just hanging out reading together or putting up our Christmas tree. We had special moments where she would mess up my hair and let me put my head on her shoulder while we watched TV, or I'd snuggle up beside her when we were watching scary movies. There were nights where we would laugh until we cried over something so insignificant that I couldn't remember it a day later. And there were mornings before I was leaving for a big trip in Europe, and she would hold my hand and tell me I was going to do amazing. But then one day she was gone: packed up and moved out. She was leaving me, the sister I never got a chance to really know. The girl I wanted to be.

She went off to live her own life, start something that didn't have the word "gymnastics" in it, and begin down a path that would let her be her own person, the independent young woman that could take on the world. No longer would she be surrounded by my name, my training, my life, and everyone always asking about me and how I was doing and where I was flying off to next. No one in this new place of hers knew me, no one would be constantly reminding her that I was the gymnast and she wasn't. I was so happy for her, and we became closer. I was fifteen and she was nineteen, ages where we could finally understand each other. But without the convenience of living together, we realized quickly that if we didn't make an effort to talk, we never would. We would lose each other. That was the last thing we wanted, even though we were so different and hadn't been close in the past. We were still sisters, and wanted the best for each other. I was so scared she was going to go away and come back a completely different person; or that she wouldn't come back at all. And I was worried that she would get into trouble or meet the wrong kind of guy.

I had nothing to worry about. She was extremely successful at university, graduating with honours, and she fell in love with one of the greatest guys I've ever known, and moved back to Toronto with a full heart. She went back to school, always wanting to learn and read, to open her mind; and she began a new life as a teacher. I smile looking at her now, so grown up, so secure with herself; and I remember when she came home that first holiday break from university. We sat on my bedroom floor and she told me she loved him. Almost ten years later, she is still with the guy she met and fell in love with, Kyle. And they're the epitome of a real couple. Kyle has become such a part of our family that I can't remember a time when he wasn't there. He's been so fully integrated that Sunday dinners aren't the same if he's not at the table talking business with my dad or picking on me. Family vacations and big events are planned around his schedule too. We love him. He is one of us, and I am so grateful that Victoria found him and has this incredible man in her life. The last few years have been rocky, and he has been there by her side to navigate the storm. Not once has he faltered. He is the steady hand on top of hers at the wheel, guiding her towards calmer waters. And I thank him for that. There is no one else that can do that, no one else that she trusts wholeheartedly, who she's willing to show her most vulnerable side to. If she didn't have that outlet, I don't know if we would still be as close as we are. He was her release.

Between missing the 2004 Olympic Games and retiring after finally making it to the 2008 Olympics in Beijing, there were four years of our lives where anywhere we went and anyone we met, my career would come up. My parents' friends, and all their friends, wanted to meet me, so intrigued by this young girl in this obscure sport. Over and over it would be the topic of discussion: "Tell us about your last trip, your last competition, how hard you train, how you manage school and sport..." and they went on and on. There would be welcome back parties, congratulation parties, going away parties. We celebrated every milestone, every big success; and not just by my family, but my friends, my club, my school, and the community. With all the press and media that hounded me, the news stories in the paper or on TV— my face was all over the place. I did speaking engagements and guest appearances. It was turning into a soap opera. Through it all, my sister was always there, supporting my every step forward, even after falling back a few. But I never saw it from her perspective. I never put my feet in her shoes and tried to see it from her side. I wasn't thinking. I wasn't even aware that maybe, just maybe, it was hard for her.

You don't want to see it. You never want to think that something that you're doing is hurting someone else. I never wanted that to happen. I never wanted my success and my dreams to affect others, but they did, and there was nothing I could do about it. Anytime someone would come up to my sister and ask her if she was the gymnast, I would cringe a little bit more. The amount of questions she got from everyone about me, all the time, must have been infuriating. Not to say she wasn't proud of me, because she was, and I know that. She wanted me to achieve the world. She was hoping and praying for it. But the endless focus on me must have been exhausting for her. It was all about Alex. When was it going to be her turn? I was torn. I wanted to be proud of my accomplishments, but ended up downplaying them instead. My family and friends bragged about me and threw all the parties, but I would never broadcast my success. Never rub it in her face or anyone else's. I became very cautious of talking about myself, which is why I'm as humble as I am today. I never wanted to make people feel inferior or jealous. I would never want people resenting me and who I had become. Deep down in my heart I know that there has to be some of that in her. She will deny this, I know she will, but it was my worst fear that she felt like she was in the shadows. I know that there had to be moments in our lives where she just desperately wanted to be recognized like I was. And she deserved to be. My career, my athletic "persona" got so big, so overwhelming that it overshadowed her amazing accomplishments. To be compared to an Olympic athlete every day of your life, to be the sibling that never liked competing—I can't imagine how difficult that would have been. It hurts me to know that she could have been hurt that I missed her graduation because I was competing at national championships, or that people may have thought less of her because she wasn't like me. And the worst part is that it was because of my choice that we turned out this way. It was my desire, my drive to do the unthinkable that caused this.

That is something that I will live with for the rest of my life.

If I had to tell my sister one thing, it would be that I would have given it all up for her. If she had asked me, if she had wanted it to be over, it could have been. But she never would have. She saw the power I had inside of me, and she saw how special that was. She kept her mouth shut and took it all in stride, never complaining in front of me once. She was the best sister that I could have ever asked for. I would have shown her that I didn't care about all the recognition, I didn't want it. I would have told her that there were days where I would have killed for no one to know anything about me. It was exhausting talking about one part of my life endlessly. That wasn't who I was, it's what I did. My sport didn't define me, the Olympics wasn't going to be the only thing I ever worked towards. But I would always be her little sister. I would always be the one that she could count on for anything. She was and always will be my biggest supporter and fan. I would give my life for her. Victoria has a light inside of her that draws people in, and a talent that should not be wasted.

Do not waste your talents. Try the unthinkable, do the impossible, reach the heights that I know you want to reach. You have it inside of you to do it. Even if you fail, you tried. You took that first step, you jumped. The courage to put yourself out there is at your fingertips. Take it and run with it.

You said we'd never lose it
You stood there and promised that to me
With those deceiving eyes you made me believe
How could I have been so stupid?

You said we'd never lose it
But you never really meant it
With those few words I fell so far
Admit that you enjoyed it

You said we'd never lose it
Lose what? I'd like to know
Thank you for opening up my eyes
I'll never forget your charming way with lies

Chapter 9:
Just Pencil Me In

I never thought that I would find someone that thought I was worth it. For years I was always second best to a teammate, to a friend, to some girl that was a better choice. It weighs on you, that constant feeling of inadequacy, that you're too much to handle, too complicated, too hard. There are a thousand pretty girls who are normal, funny and beautiful. Those girls who are on time and say things they mean; the ones that know how to take care of a man. They hold his hand and blush at his compliments. They are perfect to bring home to mom and show off to your friends. No drama. I know these girls. They're my friends, my co-workers, and my teammates. They breeze through life, easily able to commit and open themselves to someone, bringing them into their life. I'm in awe of these people. For as long as I can remember I wanted to be that girl; and somewhere along the way I lost that.

Call me crazy or commitment phobic, but twenty-four years later, and I've never found it—a real relationship, something healthy and normal—despite years where I waited for my knight in shining armour to sweep me off my feet and love me for who I am: big curly hair, Sicilian nose and all. But I was invisible; not even on the radar. I watched the boys I secretly had a crush on swoon over my pretty, tall and thin friends. I didn't understand what was so different about me. But I looked at myself in the mirror and saw I was different. For years I envied the girls I went to school with, the typical pretty girls who always wore the right clothes and said the right things, the cool kids, the girls that all the boys loved; and you'd do anything to be one of the chosen ones who sat at their lunch table. Always the shortest one in my class, I was the tomboy with the buck teeth. I cringe a little bit when I see her in my head. She had bigger eyebrows than any 12-year-old kid should have, much-needed braces, and a sense of style that no one could really put their finger on. But I didn't care that I was different. I was full of life, running at a mile a minute everywhere. Sometimes when I'm sitting with my mom at the kitchen table reminiscing over a glass of wine about little Alex, we can hear her laugh. The sound that could come out of someone so small was phenomenal. One of those laughs that comes straight from the belly and seemed to echo off the walls. Head thrown back, she committed her whole body to it. The school yard drama seemed so pointless to her. She knew who she was.

In the years that followed, I got caught up in the insecurities and fears of young girls everywhere, and doubted myself. These are those tricky years when you're coming into your own, making mistakes, hopefully picking yourself up and persevering, but getting stuck in quicksand. It's hard to grow up around girls who don't look like you. I went through a period of waking up an hour early and straightening my thick, black curly hair to look like everyone else. I bought sweatpants where they did, and wore them the way they did. But it was never really the same. Something was off, as if I was playing dress up. It didn't help that I was thin but muscular. My hair would always start to curl even when I ironed it with an actual iron. And why for some reason I never touched my big eyebrows, is beyond me. I was that awkward girl that didn't quite know she was awkward. I was the jock, the athlete that would race the boys, but then sit with the girls at the lunch table and listen to the gossip. I forgot how cruel girls could be, and I'm so lucky I was never a victim of their little games. I slid through school unscathed, getting away with it because I had the cool factor of travelling the world and bringing back medals from international tournaments. No one could make fun of that. But it didn't help me with the opposite sex. Being a female athlete and attempting any semblance of a relationship was hard; and it

Breaking Through My Limits

was hard for the rest of my career. The schedule, the travelling, the training, the prioritizing. Whenever a guy would sarcastically say, "Just pencil me in," I knew it was over. They could never understand my life or want to put up with it. What is it about a busy, strong, independent woman that is so terrifying? I went through school with one thing on my mind: the Olympics. I was so focused on sport that everything else came second. But I can't lie and say there wasn't a part of me that wanted a boy to look at me like I was the only girl in the room. The clichéd weak-in-the-knees feeling from a glance. There was that empty feeling in the pit of my stomach that craved the normalcy of dating; but at a young age I already knew it wasn't going to be easy for me. I was always the girl with a ton of guy friends, giving them advice about the girls that they wanted to date, tried to date, and were dating. I became the insider among all my friends, knowing everything about everyone, holding on to the secrets like a gatekeeper, and living vicariously through them. To them, I was the elusive single friend, fully aware of what was going on in the heads of tough, guarded boys and indecisive, playful girls. I was fascinated with my older sister and how easily the whole interacting with the opposite sex was for her. Boys loved her. They would hang on her every word, and drop by the house to come get her unexpectedly. In my eyes they were the perfect guys, and I found myself completely in love with one of them. She was the epitome of sexy. I never thought I would have the kind of power that she had. There was a time where I didn't even know if I had it in me. I stood in front of mirrors horrified at my flat chest and baby face. I just wanted to grow up and grow up quickly. But be careful what you wish for. The next few years I grew up real fast… but not in the way you think.

I slowly began to come into my own. You don't even realize it, it happens overnight, but you start feeling comfortable in your own skin. It could have been all those long nights in hotels halfway around the world, alone, tired, scared of failing. There are no luxuries for you, no decent food, nothing but water. You learn to make friends with others who don't speak your language, acclimatize yourself to new cultures and social rules. You tease people who are homesick, and you forget to call your parents because you feel as though you're living your life and not on vacation from it. Every time you get back to your old room and the routine of daily life, you're a little bit different. I became so comfortable with the fact that I was an elite athlete at fifteen, that I sacrificed a typical social life and shook off the pressure of having my country's hopes on my shoulders. You grow, learn and live.

High school started a new chapter in my life: new school, new look. To be honest, I can't say it was a complete transformation as I was still one of the smallest ones in my class, just now with braces and big eyebrows, and still no curves in sight. Training six days a week and travelling every couple of weeks for a month at a time didn't make me the obvious choice for popular girl. Olympic Qualifiers was just a few short years away, and this wasn't the time to start feeling sorry for myself. It was around this time that I started running into problems with school. My old public school was not very supportive of my athletic career and my time away from class. If I continued missing so many days during the year, they wouldn't let me graduate from high school. I remember the shock that my family experienced when we realized how difficult it was for a young elite athlete to take it to the next level, to get the support they needed to make it, and qualify for the Olympic Games. My parents knew I had to get out of there because nothing was going to make me stop training now. With Olympic Qualifiers two years away, this was crunch time. On a whim, I applied for a private school in Toronto, a place where they revelled in the fact that I was an athlete. It was a warm environment that would rally a community around me and support my efforts no matter what happened. The kicker? It was an all-girls school. My parents already believed I had no social life besides my close girlfriends anyways, so they didn't think it was a big deal. I'm pretty sure my father was rejoicing that there were no boys to deal with. Isn't it every father's dream to have a daughter who concentrates more on school and sports than on finding out just what boys were all about? He slept well at night, I'm sure.

So many reporters have asked my family to describe me in the past, and the "no social life" expression has come out in national publications on a number of occasions. I have to laugh because I'm not an antisocial girl, but I have always been an extremely private person. Guarded some would say. The mysterious, athletic, busy girl has been my M.O. ever since I got out of high school and really walked into the world of dating. No guy had really looked at me until I was about nineteen, when I had finally started morphing into a young woman. I was just a late bloomer, and I'm thankful for that because who knows if I would have given it all up? If I had been distracted with a relationship, it may have affected my attitude on long trips, my training and results. I couldn't take that risk. It meant too much to me to throw it all away. The "what ifs" will drive you insane. Maybe it was a blessing in disguise, as difficult as it was to accept, because my life may have never been the same.

To be humble and grateful for attention is admirable, respectful, and something that I've experienced and hope to demonstrate to other young women. I dated in university and met a lot of great people, but I found out quickly how some people try and use you for who you are or what you appear to be on the outside. There were former friends who loved that I was such a high-level athlete, but were so jealous they tried to sabotage me behind my back, bring me down as far as they could push me. Some boys only saw one thing that I was worth. I became so untrusting over those years, and I really was this naïve little thing looking for love, as cheesy as that sounds. I imagined I would find that perfect person that would accept my schedule and all the crazy that comes along with being with me, and we would strike this perfect balance between my career and a relationship. I never did fit that hopeless romantic typecast. Needless to say, nothing in my life has ever been easy, and the type of person I am makes things more difficult.

I'm a realist. After years of being a single girl living in a big city, I've become a harsher critic of "love" and relationships. Trust is not something that comes easily with me. I've seen countless girlfriends who have been torn up by a relationship: cheated on, lied to, and hit. An unexpected breakup can send someone over the edge. I've seen girls lie in bed unable to sleep or eat. They ache in places they didn't even know they had inside of them, devastated. Life literally stalls, and it's hard to even get out of bed in the morning. Others get angry, and throw all their morals out the window wanting to get even. They suddenly become a different person, out to hurt the other. Usually they end up hurting themselves more and ruining what little chance they might have had to get back together. I've seen it all way too many times before. The pain you feel is temporary, trust me. I went on like this for years, never really understanding what they were going through because I had never been hurt like that. I used to pride myself on that fact and breathe a sigh of relief every time I left a crying friend, thanking God it wasn't me.

I know there are people out there like me. Men and women who struggle to find a connection with someone or push those who care about them away because they're scared of getting hurt. There's distrust of what you would become if you let yourself be happy. I've been there.

And then one trip, one day, changed my whole life, and all my big philosophies and cynical outlooks went out the window. The short memories I have will always remain, every detail, every breath, every look. Years later, and it is still etched in my mind, the feeling of you on my skin, and the rain that swallowed us up.

Chapter 10:
You Said We'd Never Lose It

B y 2007 I had given up worrying about my love life. It was a lost cause, so I never went looking for it. A night out wouldn't end with a new number in my cell and a perfect start to a relationship. I was so close to the Olympics I could taste it, and flying down to South America for possibly my last multi-sport event, I let my mind wonder about what this trip had in store for me. I secretly hoped that maybe, just maybe, this would be the trip that would change my life. And for the first time, I was right.

Everyone is so curious about the athletes' village at a major Games, and my friends would always want all the gossip and details of the latest relationship or cutest team. They were always so envious that I was surrounded by the world's best athletes in a place that seemed like adult camp to all of them. I can't help but admit that it's kind of true. The village is the best part of any Games. It's a community and a family, but also a place that can take your mind off your nerves or a horrible practice. There are distractions that can take you far away from your doubts, or if you need a pick-me-up after a loss. The beauty of it is that we can all relate to each other, which is so hard to find when you're back in the real world trying to make people understand what you're dealing with. If you haven't lived it, you're not going to get it. I'm not saying that all my friends who supported me over the years didn't help me, but there are things that you can share with an athlete that sound crazy to a typical 20-year-old back home.

Coming from an individual sport, I thrived on being a part of Team Canada and having dozens of us all together sharing an apartment building dripping with Canadian pride. It was such a unique experience and an honour to be a part of so many Games, and I looked forward to them every year. I was counting down the days till we boarded that flight to Rio. We flew down with a few other teams, and already the stress in my chest was beginning to lift. It was the interaction with other athletes heading into a major Games that kept your spirits up. It was infectious. The first few days in the village, and I was feeling good. I was in the best shape of my career, and had a newfound confidence and energy vibrating out of me that everyone around me could feel.

It was a fluke that I even saw him. Running out of the medical centre on the second floor, late for practice, I headed straight for the stairs as there was no sense in waiting for the elevator. Out of the corner of my eye he was standing there at the elevator doors, probably heading up to his room, definitely not in any rush. I remember thinking, "Who is that? And why haven't I seen him before?" As I jolted down the stairs and met up with my teammates, I couldn't help but smile. I was going to need to meet that one.

The next few days of getting ready for competition were a blur. I hung out with a lot of great people and made some incredible friends, but this mystery guy was nowhere to be found. Then I would see him in passing or walking with a group, but never long enough to even say anything. Why was I nervous? It seemed so crazy to me that I needed to meet someone so badly, but kept missing my opportunity. There was more than enough to keep me occupied with my competition coming up. We were both competing at the same time, and the days were flying by. My experiences at those Games were some of the most intense, competitive moments of my career. After I survived being disqualified, having to watch someone take the title I had worked so hard for, and then come back and win three gold medals to be our flag bearer—I was mentally and physically drained. It was easily one of the worst and best moments of my life. I ran into him the night I won my three gold, expecting to go celebrate with a big plate of dessert, then head to bed. But he wanted me to come out that night, escape the village and go celebrate with a big group of athletes. Canada had won so many medals in those last couple of days, and there was more than enough reason to celebrate. I couldn't say no to him.

It was pouring rain that night, and not the kind of rainy day I was used to. It was this otherworldly kind of rain that looked like sheets of water enveloping us. Group by group, people dashed out running to the gates where cabs were waiting to take us downtown. It was like running through a never-ending waterfall. I jumped into a cab with three of my teammates, and those thirty minutes in the pitch dark, with the cab maneuvering through the busy streets in the heavy rain, I saw flashes of the three of us lost in the slums of Rio. My pulse was racing until we stopped, and there was a huge group of athletes from all over the world packed under an awning, waiting to get into a dark building. I have never been so happy to step out into the pouring rain. We were all packed like sardines under this little tent, the music pounding every time the door opened to let more of us in, one by one. The line was moving slowly, and I leaned into him in line. These are the things that you hope will lead to something more, a sign or a small gesture that makes you feel as though you're not in this alone. He leaned into me, and that was all I needed. From the minute we walked through the door, we didn't leave each other's side. His hand on my back, my body pressed up against his. It was steamy and hot, and we made our way to the dance floor brushing up against the wet skin all around us. We danced for what seemed like hours, my arms wrapped around his neck, synching our bodies. He pulled me close. All I could see was him. I smiled, eyes shut, head tilted up towards him, hair thrown back as his head bent downwards towards mine. He laughed. I hadn't kissed someone in so long. He didn't believe me. I wouldn't lie.

I was in a daze that night, lost all track of time, stuck in the moment with him.

He held my hand and for the first time I didn't want to let go. In the early hours of the morning, we were one of the last ones to come back to the village, safe within the guarded walls.

We passed through security and stared at that crazy rain that just wouldn't let up. It was like a scene out of a movie. We had quite a way to run until we got to our building, so we braced ourselves, he grabbed my hand and ran. Halfway there I lost my flip flop, and breaking from our group, I had to go back and get it. Soaking wet, exhausted from dancing all night, I broke from him and turned around. At this point I couldn't help but hysterically laugh. The only light that shone was coming from the lampposts lining the pathway back to our rooms. The night swallowed us up, and you could only see one foot in front of you as the rain was so thick. He came with me and I slipped on my shoe. We weren't concerned with catching up to everyone ahead of us. We were only concerned with that second, that first time alone together wrapped in darkness, standing underneath a waterfall. He stepped in and took my hands. We interlaced our fingers effortlessly and stood there smiling at each other. It was just the two of us. He put his arms around me, holding my hands behind my back, inching closer and closer ever so slowly until he leaned in and kissed me. I shut my eyes lightly and sunk into his lips, tasting him. If he wasn't holding me, my knees would have given out completely, lost in this dream world where the lines of reality became so blurred. I could live in that moment forever.

He had opened up something inside me and I wasn't quite sure what it was. I held his hand to let people know that I was his, even if it was just for that moment. I didn't want to leave him. I don't know how it had happened, but I cared about him and wanted him to remember that this was different, pure. The next day we would fly back home and leave all of this behind us, the magic, the touch of my fingers on his face. It was dangerous to be with him there, he made me feel like a completely different person. When it was time for me to go to the airport, I didn't want to leave him, and thought it was crazy for even thinking that. I barely knew him. Two days was all it took, all I needed. We sat down in some quiet, private spot that day, out of sight. We just sat there, our arms entangled, my head on his shoulder, his skin on mine. He took a picture of us, me in my shades as usual, and I kissed him. I flew those ten hours home, and I actually missed him. I hoped he wouldn't forget me.

But you didn't. I had never been happier, and my girlfriends who were used to my bitter and sarcastic demeanour when it came to boys, were shocked. They all wanted to meet this mystery guy who had brought me to life. I grew so much with you even in such a short time. I had never really dated anyone I really cared for, and I didn't know what I was doing. I was so young and had fallen so fast. The first time we saw each other again when we were back home I was scared you would realize that I wasn't anything special after all. I drove myself crazy until I saw you, and was relieved. It was just right. After dinner it was a beautiful night, and with neither one of us wanting to go home, we walked all the way downtown. It was one of those gorgeous, cool August nights. We rode the subway back uptown to your car. I laugh when I think back to us then. We all of a sudden were meeting the parents. Dinner with your dad so early on would have usually sent me running, but this time I knew I wanted to. I had never done the parents thing before. He was a former athlete too, and such a warm man. I remember trying to see you in him, in the subtle way he cooked and used his hands when he talked. I felt a part of your life. Our friends thought we were crazy. I can't explain it. It just happened.

But I was heading for a six-week trip that was the most important of my athletic career. I had this horrible feeling rising in my chest that this would be the end of this picture-perfect fairytale we were living. I pushed it as far down as I could and tried to tell myself I was getting worked up over nothing. This last European tour had me competing in four different cities and ending with a training camp before heading to Olympic Qualifiers in Greece. That was it. That trip could have very well been the end of my career, and it was my time to see what I was capable of, and put it all on the line. We threw a big going away party for me at the house, with a big family barbecue. Everyone knew that this was my last shot, but no one really wanted to say it. My friends and family all gathered to support me, but everyone wanted to meet you: the boy that Alex actually fell for. As the night came to an end, the music became softer and mellower. The wine glasses were piling up, and people were avoiding the kitchen to stop eating. The few troopers sat outside on that cool August night wrapped up in blankets, with the light from a few candles illuminating our faces. You held my hand within my little cocoon, and we were happy then. I waited for a moment alone with you on our last night together. The talking turned to quiet chatter, and eventually people went silent. It had been a long night. With the last candle burning out, we all got up to go inside and say our goodbyes. They wished me luck and filled me with so much love, hoping it would carry me through the next few weeks. I sat on the couch, wrapped up in you, and you played with my hands as always. You traced my fingers with yours, pushing down on my nails with your thumb. I would know your touch just from that. I would recognize it anywhere. One of my girlfriends decided to stay, and sat across from us talking into the early hours of the morning until she finally went home. I closed the door behind her and sleepwalked back to the couch, sliding into the small nook that you had left for me. We managed to fit on that small couch, overheating from the suede that we were sunk into. You pulled me in so tight, and I could feel your breath lightly, rocking me to sleep. I knew you had to go, but I didn't want you to. I had this sinking feeling that we had just fallen into quicksand. You kissed me goodbye that morning and gave me our first pictures together to remember you by while I flew halfway around the world. It brought Brazil back to me as I stood in my doorway about to embark on the biggest journey of my life. You left, and promised me you would be there when I got back.

But so much changed over those six weeks. I didn't meet someone new or lose the feelings I had for you, but my life changed and I had to change with it. After a gruelling trip of training camps and competitions all over Europe, I qualified for the Olympic Games at the World Championships in Patras, Greece. In that one moment, I had gotten everything I had ever wanted. The millisecond it took to flash my name in the top ten on the scoreboard was all it took. The years of struggling, of pain and heartbreak were gone—a memory of a past that I would never have to look back on again because I had done it. All I could see was the future, and all I could do was look forward. Before I could even celebrate, I was in meetings. Now that qualifying was out of the way, the goal was to increase my ranking, make the final at the Olympics, and plan out how I was going to do that. The pressure hit me before I could even blink an eye. My coach was moving out to Spain the next week, and what would happen to me? I had to be there to train with her, but I couldn't risk my preparation for Beijing. I didn't think twice about it. I was there, and was going to be there most of the next year leading up to the Games. I had never thought about what would actually happen if I qualified. It was all about getting there first. The microscope that I was now going to be put under was even worse than I could imagine. I spent a week thinking about you and how this wasn't going to work. I put it in my head that dragging you through this wasn't something I wanted to do. I was still battling with my body image issues, and getting ready to sacrifice everything for the next year, set on focusing only on myself. I needed to get my head back together and figure out how I was going to tackle the next few months without having a complete breakdown. This was everything I had wanted, and I desperately wanted it to be a perfect ending. So I came home and got up the nerve to break your heart. I told you I couldn't bring you along for the roller coaster that would be my life the next year. The ups were great, but you didn't understand how low the downs were. I would never have wanted you to see me that way, ever. There were dark days where I wouldn't even recognize myself or know who I was. This horrible person comes out inside you that you want to hide away from the world; the demons you have inside scratching to get out, and they do. I was scared I was going to let you in and you were going to run away as fast as you could once you saw the real me. The buzz from Brazil was too perfect to keep up, and we wouldn't have been able to keep that up once I was back at training. But you fought for us. You didn't understand how I could throw it away. What you never could understand was that I was doing it for you, trying to be so strong. You deserved a girl who would be there for you, who would appreciate you, who would be the girlfriend by your side. I couldn't be her. I was leaving for Spain in a few weeks, and all I could concentrate on was how I was going to make it work: my coach out in Europe, me living here training alone. It scared me that I wasn't going to live up to the expectations that had been set for me, and that after such a great year in 2007, I was going to lose it, go down instead of up. I didn't know how to handle it, and I didn't let you help me. I know now that you just wanted to be there for me so I didn't face it all alone, but I chose to do it by myself. I hurt you.

Life resumed. I pushed you as far from my mind as I could, but I was seeing you everywhere: at the mall, at concerts, at the Starbucks near my house. You were constantly in my thoughts. I didn't know if this was some sort of sign or punishment for hurting you, and I was counting down the days till I left for Spain to spend ten hours a day training, and nothing else. I needed to escape this place that reminded me so much of you because I wouldn't be able to stay so strong. I never wanted to be the girl that would mess with your head, making it impossible for you to get over me. But in the end I didn't actually want you to move on. I wanted you to wait for me.

I got back from that first long haul in Spain, and for the first time in a long time, felt sure of myself. I stopped thinking that my coach moving away was the worst thing that could have ever happened to me. I let go of some of that pressure I was carrying and looked forward to the new year. 2008 was THE year. The year I had been waiting for. It was a funny feeling to actually be waking up in 2008 knowing that for the last four years, this was the year I had dreamed of. The next six months were it, and I was happy. I wanted you to be a part of my life, and I sucked up my pride and called you. The sound of your voice made me calm. I wanted to see you. We met. It felt like years had passed when I saw you walking towards me. You were different, guarded, yet still the same. We walked the cold streets to a little place I knew, and grabbed a seat. The lighting was dark, darker than I remembered. I leaned in over the candle, placing my hands around the glass holder trying to get warm. We made the typical small talk that all conversations start out with before someone hits you with something heavy, and we both knew it was coming, you must have. I looked at you and told you the only thing I would ever regret is letting you go. I did it for a reason, and I apologized over and over again, so many times my lips were sick of saying it. I never thought that I made the wrong decision, but I never wanted to let you go. I sat across from you and poured my heart out, put it all on the line because I didn't know what else to do. I wanted you by my side. You told me you still felt the same way and knew that I would come back to you. As you spoke you looked so pained, so torn up, and I knew something bad was coming. You couldn't even look at me. You said that if I came back to you, you thought you would be able to walk away from whomever you were with at that time because of what I meant to you. But now that it was actually happening, it wasn't so easy. All of a sudden I was nauseous. The room starting to spin as I spat out the words I didn't even think I could say. "You were seeing someone?" I was shattered, and had to get up and leave before I couldn't pick up all the pieces of myself off the cold, hard floor. I couldn't even look at you, and walked in front trying to hail a cab. I didn't want you to see me cry. You jumped in my cab and I sat as far away from you as I could, pressed up against the door so you could see my breath on the window. You tried to get me to look at you, but I wouldn't let myself. I knew I had to say goodbye, but that word seemed so final, so life changing at the time. I jumped out of the cab without saying goodbye, and you didn't let me go like that. You pulled me into your arms on that freezing cold corner, and we were stuck like that, frozen in time. You kissed my forehead, and I broke away from you, heading home in a daze.

Those are the moments when you think that you've never been as hurt as you were then. Putting myself back there makes me ache. What if one decision, one choice changed your life forever? I believe that life is full of pathways, and you can choose to go one way or another that can lead you to a completely new road. There's no right or wrong choice, but a different life waiting for you at the end of the tunnel. If you take what happens to you in stride, keep your head up and know that there will be another clearing sometime soon, you'll never think about the what ifs. There are no what ifs in life. You live it, you make the choices. Even the ones that may end up hurting you are there to take you to a better place. A place to learn and grow. A place that you were meant to end up. Every door that closes opens a new one. It's so hard to see that when you're standing in the middle of a crossroads, when you have one foot in the past and one in the future. You know you need to move forward and take that new path, but you're stuck. You feel suffocated, lifeless. Straddling two lives but not living one. That is exactly how I felt. I wanted nothing and everything to do with you. I wanted to hate and love you at the same time. My pride was fighting that weak side in me that just wanted to go back a few months ago and never let you out of my sight. I was so angry I couldn't sleep. You were supposed to be the one that was there with open arms, forgiving me. But you weren't. You showed up at my door that week and I wanted to slam it in your face. But you were my kryptonite. We sat in your car and I let you hold my hand. I knew you were with someone else, but I needed your touch. We talked and talked, but nothing seemed to change. You were so conflicted, trying to figure out what to do. Do you leave this perfect, easy girl for the one who hurt you? The girl who stomped on your heart and ran away to Europe, disappearing off the face of the earth for months? Do you take a risk and fall, or play it safe? I could see your mind going a million miles a minute. I told you I couldn't see you if you were still with her because that wasn't fair to anyone. You didn't even have to touch me for us to feel bad. We were magnetic. Even if you pulled us apart we always found our way back to each other.

You took a risk and said you ended things, which didn't go

well. No one had ever broken up with someone for me before, and it wasn't as easy as I thought it would be. It was awful actually. Someone gave up on something good, great even, for me. I never asked him to, but if we were going to see each other, that was how it was going to be. You came over, exhausted, upset and so indifferent. Telling someone it was over for no apparent reason was hard enough, but for her to take it so badly was even worse. She fought for you, cried. I didn't want to know and I didn't care. I didn't want to know about her, all I wanted was you. Things were actually going to work out, and I really believed that. I thought it would be hard for you to deal with hurting another girl, and it was. You were there, but not all there. I refused to see it, and let my imagination run away with me as I fantasized about us being the way we were before. It was all a dream. When I think back to how caught up I was in the situation, it makes me nauseous. I had great people in my life, but all I could see was you. You left for a trip, and we talked every day into the late hours of the night. I missed you. Everything seemed to be going fine, and I thought that maybe the drama had finally left us. I couldn't have been more wrong.

Just when you think everything is going alright, something happens to make you rethink it all. I remember getting a call from a friend asking about you, and I remember thinking that was weird. My friend had happened to come across some photos of you. I will never forget this night, scared to click my mouse, knowing exactly what was going to pop up on my screen. I didn't think I had the stomach for it. There you two were, images that I'll never forget.

I would never believe anything that came out of your mouth ever again. That was it for us. I was so disgusted. We didn't speak for months. All I could see every time I thought of you were your lips on her cheek, her blonde hair. You ended up with someone my exact opposite: petite, blonde, perfect. The girl I always wanted to be, but would never be. I began to think that everything we had was all a figment of my imagination. It wasn't real, you were pretending. Everything became fake in my head: your words, your moves, the way you looked at me. I didn't know what to believe anymore. As tough as I was trying to be, I knew I came out of it so damaged. I would never trust another guy ever again, never let anyone close to me because I refused to let someone make me feel that way again. I had more than my share of pressure to be better than I was, to live up to a potential that people placed on me. I lived every day of my life thinking I wasn't good enough, and I didn't need a boy to think the same. I was better than that. I deserved better.

A month or two before the Olympics, you appeared in my life, like clockwork. Every four to six months you would show up to check in, make sure I hadn't fully moved on. As great as it was to hear from you, I was always more than willing to push the limits of a friendly conversation. I was curious as to why you would want to talk to me out of the blue. Our conversations could get heated, emotional; and I've learned anything to do with us is usually like that. We could never just talk, it always got personal. It was always dangerous. Slowly but surely you would suck me back in, even when I fought it. I thought I had everything under control, but with you I never could control myself. We all have those people in our lives, certain people that can make you throw everything you stand for out the window.

I tried to keep my guard up with you, that fake wall I stood behind that you could knock right over with your hand on my back. You never thought that I would go out of my way to be with you, that I could think of someone else for a change. You knew that my focus was on my athletic career, clearly. That was never the problem as that was what drew us together. We got what the other was going through, athlete to athlete, no explaining, and no keeping it in. I got it. You got it. It was our lives. You never had to feel bad about being frustrated or disappointed. I wasn't going to baby you or tell you that everything was going to be okay. I was going to push you, tell you to work harder, try and get more out of you. I can challenge you like no one else can. You were the one that said that to me. But there I was, drove out of my way to see you, the first time in months and the last time before I left for the Olympics. I was back at that house eating dinner in your dining room with your father a year ago. It was a sick déjà vu, and I remember thinking how fast time had flown by. We sat watching TV on separate ends of the couch, not quite sure what I was expecting or what was running through your head. What were we doing? I was doing nothing wrong, you wanted to see me, I wanted to see you. I just figured you would never put us in a situation like that when you were still attached to her. I didn't even think to ask, I just assumed. I always assumed with you, even when I knew I shouldn't. To sleep at night I had to. It was always so perfect in our own little cocoon: the safety of a private place, a private world. We time-travelled back to a place that we both wished we could find our way back to, somehow. I lay with my head on your chest, rising up and down in a soothing rhythm, trying to watch a movie. I closed my eyes and just let our bodies sync. "Don't let yourself fall again. Don't let yourself fall again," I repeated over and over in my head. But looking up at him from that angle, tracing the lines of his cheekbones and the contours of his face with my eyes—I was too far gone. He walked me to my car, slowly. I was leaving in the next few days, so this was it. Another trip, another excuse for us to never be together. He kissed me goodbye. I thought maybe this time it would be different. Maybe after a year we would be able to figure it all out and leave the past behind us. I felt like you led me on, you made me believe it was possible. The messages from back home you sent me while I was away, the little gestures that made me trust in you again. You would think a girl would learn. You told me I was the only girl you thought you could ever love. I'll never know if you meant it.

What killed me is that even though you never trusted me to be with me again, you were the one that understood me the best, the one I wanted to go to when I was dealing with something I couldn't handle. You were the one person that I didn't care if you knew what I was scared of. I wanted to tell you the things that I keep deep down inside, and I reached out for your shoulder to lean on. And it was always there, every single time. You knew me the best, and I hated that. Those are the people that always hurt you the most in the end. And you did.

Months would pass with no communication, only for one of us to cave in and contact the other. Back and forth we played this little game. You are the definition of playing with fire. It always ends badly, but you can't help but risk it. My mother always scolded me for running my fingers quickly through the hot flame that lit up the dining room table. My sister sat smugly across from me, mocking me for even trying. "How many times do you have to burn your fingers before you stop reaching for it?" she would ask. I smiled at her, there was just something dangerous about it, playing with matches, watching the older kids burn paper, and whatever else they thought they could control. But that's the thing about fire, you think you can control it, but you never can. It has a mind of its own, twisting and turning in ways you never thought possible. It can grow so out of your control that in the blink of an eye it's destroying everything in its path. But that's the chance you're always willing to take.

Every word that I message you is like pulling the match out of the box, ever so slowly. Your charming digs spark, but no cigar, until the eventual, casual drink, and that first glance strikes it hot. How far we want to take it depends on how long we can burn. The more we play the hotter it gets, but someone always puts out the flame before it all comes crashing down around us. We're smarter than I once thought. One day we'll both get burned, but we're waiting for it.

You changed me, made me stronger, tougher, thicker skinned. It didn't hurt when I didn't hear from you anymore; but when I did, I took it for what it was. And now after all these years and all this time that has passed, I can't remember who we used to be. We try so desperately to hold on to the people we once were, but we're not them anymore. Some days I get a glimpse of the past, a flicker of something so pure before everything fell apart. Now you're the one that I know is always there, but shouldn't be. I would never expect anything from you. When I'm with you I still feel something, but always have to stop myself, a defense mechanism. There's a wall that goes up now, trying to keep you away from my heart because nothing will ever really change, and I won't put myself through that ever again. I have to walk away, and you have to let me go.

There are people in the world that fought for me, fought for something real, something that I couldn't see because you were standing in front of me. You can't show me that fight anymore, it was lost a long time ago. Somewhere in there I know that we will always care about each other, always want the best as we grow up and move on, but I know I won't be the one walking beside you when it's all over. Lives change, cities change, feelings change. I have always just wanted you to be true to yourself and stop living in denial with what you really want.

No one should make you feel like a consolation prize, a "special" second best. There are things in life you so desperately want to believe, to hold on to a feeling, a moment, or a few precious months when you were so happy. But letting them go gives you the space inside of yourself to let someone else create even stronger memories. Different ones, but real, honest and true. It isn't about replacing the experiences that you once shared with someone, but moving them so you can see past them. I was scared of losing him, losing that feeling forever and not finding it again. But if someone cares about you they wouldn't hurt you so much. I fell in love with the boy I met years ago, but he's not that person anymore, and I'm not that girl. It took a long time to realize it, but when you finally do, you can walk away with no regrets. Heartbroken maybe, but finally able to heal.

You can't keep living in a jaded dream world. You're hurting people, but most of all you're hurting yourself. Don't be scared to fail and know how much potential you have. If you say you want something, then go and do it, don't hold back and make excuses. I hate the word "maybe". You know what you're capable of. You'll either do something, or you won't.

Chapter 11:
Losing Friends, Finding Family

Most of my life I have watched people come in and out of my world, with those special few that stick. My friends have always been such a huge part of my being, a secret source of happiness and comfort. I have been fortunate to have people that I could lean on at all stages of my life, people that went out of their way to help me or show me the way. With my success in sport and a career that took off at such a young age, I have also, unfortunately, known people who I thought were my friends, who I thought were there for me, but never really were. People I trusted, that I let into my life, who turned their back on me. I never thought it was possible to turn so cold so quickly, for a person to do a complete one eighty. And each time it happened it shocked me, shocked me to see how little respect they had for me in the end.

You never believe that someone could say such horrible things to your face, or even worse, behind your back. Spread malicious lies and rumours that are created just to hurt you, with no other purpose. Revenge, jealousy, or just pure entertainment, I never understand why people do the things they do. What possesses a person to so easily sabotage someone they once called a friend? Unfortunately, since I was young, I've dealt with these kinds of situations too many times. The half friends: Those that hold on tight, only to try and squeeze out every ounce of your energy. Thankfully, I've also been lucky to have met some of the most incredible people, who no matter what, always stood beside me. Those few people that understand your craziness, your weird little things that you don't let anyone else see. The people that you can act like you're a kid again with and not worry that someone is going to judge you. These are people who care about you, who want the best for you and will always go out of their way to help you through. These are the keepers. They're the keepers of my secrets, my dreams, my darkest thoughts. They are the beautiful things in my life, and I smile every day, thankful to have their love and their light.

I moved through grade school pretty unscathed; and being an athlete helped. I was never the popular one, but never bullied. When I needed to find a new school that was more supportive of my athletic career, I never thought I would have to make new friends again, to walk into an environment where I was even more different than before and hopefully find people who would let me in. I was so angry at my parents for wanting me to switch schools, to leave all my friends behind. It was all I had known. It was comfortable, easy. You knew your place, your friends, the histories, the relationships. But I knew that to do what I wanted to do in the next few years, I needed to go and find a school that would help me graduate and get to the Olympics. A school that would make sure that I would get the education I needed and not hinder my athletic performance. My new high school was the perfect fit, but stepping into an all-girls private school from years in the co-ed public system was a nightmare. This was a completely new beast. Everything I thought I knew, I didn't. Everything I was expecting, wasn't even close. The girls, the money, the attitudes—it was surreal. The financial burden my sport had put on my family made me realize how thankful I was to have the support that I did. Trendy clothes and labels were the last thing that I would ask for, and I would never beg my parents for the latest toy or designer purse. I was never materialistic like that. Then I pulled those green knee-high socks on, tightened my tie and strolled into the hallowed halls where I would spend the next four years. I was so quiet that year, so out of my element, so unsure of being myself and having these girls understand me. But because the Olympics was getting closer, all of a sudden it felt like the girls who probably would never have given me a second look, were being so friendly. When they understood exactly what I was doing with my life outside the locker room, there were invites to parties and shopping trips. As we got older and I witnessed my friends' first foray into drinking and drugs, I knew I wasn't ready for that. I had a real shot at something outside of being a normal teenager, and I pushed away from them. It was an easy transition that they let happen. No one stopped me or tried to include me in their wild ways. We had grown up in two different directions, and they knew it, and so did I. I could have walked a thin line and let myself fall into that scene, party every weekend and experiment, push the boundaries. I sometimes wonder what my life would have been like if I hadn't stepped away, if I had stayed within that tight group of girls. Would I have quit after I missed the Olympics the first time around? I don't know, and I'll never know. However, I do know that I wouldn't be the person I am today, and maybe I'd have gone off in a completely different direction. I might have wanted to go away to university like they all did, and give up my career because my priorities would have been different.

When the summer of 2004 came and went, the Olympics, my Olympics, passed me by. I sat on my couch watching girls that I should have been competing against become Olympians. It was excruciating. What was worse was to walk into classes at the start of Grade 12 and have to tell everyone that I didn't go to the Olympics. I wasn't good enough. Everything I had ever worked for didn't actually happen. Every day it got worse, like taking a bullet each time. I was different because of it, and they all were towards me. It was a combination of pity, sadness and disappointment. Or at least it felt like that to me. My life had changed, and I was changed because of it. There was a girl who had her locker next to mine since Grade 9. Our last names were always paired next to each other even with new girls coming in every year, and we were always together. That last year of high school, we suddenly started to become closer. I was introduced to so many new people through her, and slowly slipped away from my old life and friends into this new circle, this new crowd. I had classes with girls I always wanted to get to know, but never did. These girls, these special girls became my core group, my best friends, my lifeline.

When I close my eyes and imagine the group of us then, we were a group of ambitious, talented young women. Every one of us so different in our own ways, so unique, but with qualities in us that made us so strong. They motivated me to get the best out of myself, and they pushed me. They were so incredibly smart that I remember being intimidated. I always received good grades even with training, but it never came that easily. I had to work and study and read all the time. If I fell behind, it was disastrous. But they never seemed to hit a hiccup along the way. They stressed like all Grade 12 students do when applying for university and getting your grades up, but in the end they were all at the top of their class. Med school, business school, law school—we killed ourselves to get the grades that would propel us into our future. A high powered future, a successful career, a profession. They were so focused, so ambitious. I had the opportunity to be around such an accomplished group of young women day in and day out that year. We became so close, sharing everything: clothes, secrets, boy stories. They would come over and we would sit around my kitchen table and talk for hours, my mom laughing at all our inside jokes and the whispering that filtered up through the vents into her bedroom. We would camp out in my living room and eat until we were exhausted. After every dance, we would end up in the kitchen, huddled around our island recounting the night's events. We thought we had such important things to discuss; such die hard issues to debate and over analyze. We would plan house parties and what we were doing on the weekends. It was a great year, and after such a disappointment in my life, they picked me back up. They calmed my nerves over coffee and chocolate, raided my fridge after a late night, and would stop by before my many big trips, with plane letters filled with words of encouragement. When we finally graduated in the summer of 2005, I was Alex again. I had my whole life in front of me.

I am a firm believer that being able to forgive is a great trait. To accept an apology, take it at face value and move forward is hard, but so important. Don't hold things in, and don't hold grudges that can eat you alive. You need to get it off your chest. However, I don't forget. Maybe that's a grudge to some people, but it's not for me. I can forgive a person, but I will never forget that in that one instance they were capable of something I never thought they could be. I will forgive someone because I know we're only human and we have insecurities and fears that make us do horrible things to others. But I won't forget that they hurt me. I won't forget that they left me out in the cold when I needed them. I can still be friends with them and salvage a relationship, but there's a piece inside of me that holds all these memories, that makes sure I know who I can trust and the type of people I really want in my life.

As I hit my quarter life crisis this year, I know the type of person I am, who I want to be and what I'm striving for. I know who loves me for me and is happy for me, not secretly jealous or envious. I know who brings my energy up, and the ones that always seem to bring me down in the end. Every year I reflect on my life and the people in it. I encourage you all to do the same. Who should you reach out to, and keep in your life? Don't let them slip away. Life is so busy and we're over stimulated, overwhelmed, over everything. It's so easy to let someone fall through the cracks, lose touch, lose hope. Don't let it happen to the ones that mean something to you, even if it's an old girlfriend or boyfriend, an ex friend. There are people that are special to you and were special for a reason. Don't let them go. Suck up your pride and put yourself out there. Make new relationships out of old ones. It is so important to surround yourself with those who get the best out of you, that make you feel like you can do anything, that make you smile.

I have lost so many friends along the way, and I know being my friend hasn't been easy sometimes. I used to cancel all the time, could never make plans at the last minute, and was dealing with so much stress and pressure that I couldn't be there for them at times. But those that dealt with it, that understood me, would have my undying attention when I could give it to them, and would always have my love. The people who put up with my moods, that let me be stubborn and try and battle things on my own, but would always come to me with open arms in the end; the people that never looked at me like I was different because of my life, of what I was trying to achieve—they are real. They are my real friends. They are and always will be my family.

I have no right to be upset
You were everything you could have been
I pushed you away
It's okay, you can say it
My greedy hands kept you at arm's length
You pushed. I pulled
A tug of war that ended with me on my knees

Was I so blind to see the faded dirt stains on your
    Harry Rosen suit?
Cuts and bruises, bites and scratches
Hidden beneath your collared shirt
Such perfect deception
What a beautiful couple they said
Perfect on paper
The two of us walking side by side
Holding your hand seemed my biggest problem then

You wanted me, and I made you work for it
Played you like a little toy
Wrapped you around my little finger
You said you wouldn't let that happen, remember?

It was fun
I never thought you'd break me
I never thought I'd miss you
I've lost you now
It was me
I hurt you
Not even love could save this now
Not even a picture to show that it was real
Years will pass and there will be nothing to
    show for it

I knew you were trouble from that very first night
You gave me a rush under the stars that I'll never
    forget
You were like a drug
Something you slip into your mouth with a smile
Knowing that tomorrow it will be gone forever

Chapter 12:
Perfectly Imperfect

How is it possible that no matter how hard we fight against it, the events of our past shape our future? It's impossible to forget the worst memories: the ones you wish were just a horrible dream waking you up in the middle of the night, sweating and praying it was a figment of your imagination. The nightmares of stupid mistakes, unforgiveable words, loss. As if living through the pain in the moment wasn't hard enough, a sliver of it stays with you. A little piece of glass that slips deeper and deeper to remind you of the pain it caused. You run your fingers over it. The healed skin is a discomfort. Just when you think you've forgotten, you haven't. Your mind plays tricks on you. Sometimes it thinks it's happy until a familiar reminder creeps into your subconscious.

There are those that move through their lives phase by phase, seamlessly. People who cope with stress, disappointment, and failure. Those lucky ones that live and learn; they move on as genuinely happy people. Yes, they are out there. But it's not as easy as you think. It's shockingly fun to be bitter and cynical, and there's less chance of getting hurt. There's no commitment, no promise of good behaviour, no one to answer to. My first heartbreak didn't just break me, it tore me apart. There was no clean break, no closure, no nothing. It seemed to go on forever, and after years of being pulled and pushed and taken advantage of, I was done. I became so cold, so incapable of feeling anything for anyone. All I could see when I was with someone new was the lies, the false sense of security, or the other girl. Thanks to him, my wall went up so high that I couldn't see over it anymore, couldn't get out of my own way to see what I had right in front of me all along.

I had heard about you long before I ever saw your face. Your name permanently marked into my mind as it smoothly fell off my best friend's lips. We had just graduated from high school, and even though I knew this was going to happen, I stayed in Toronto with my coach to train while all my friends scattered to universities all over the country. I so wanted to go with them. I remember that last summer before they headed to Kingston or London or Montreal. They all split up so strategically to start a new life for themselves, a new chapter with a brand new identity to play with.

Stepping foot in residence with my packed suitcases at the University of Toronto changed everything. I fell into a world that consumed me: the excitement of the unknown, nerves, masses of new people that were all looking for somewhere to belong. It was exhilarating to have a shot to be whoever you wanted to be, and shake off that high school image for good. I came to U of T with an attitude adjustment; still that hardcore athlete, but more willing to take some risks, have a little fun, bend the rules and test these new waters. At the time, I kept telling myself that I knew my body, I knew myself. If I stay up all night, I'm still getting ready for the gym at 5 a.m. no matter what. You just do it, and nine times out of ten I felt horrible, but snapped out of it once I stepped foot at practice. Once you realize you can get away with it, this double life—you fall deeper down the rabbit hole.

My best friend was experiencing it all too, this new world out on her own a few hours away. When I would finally get a chance to catch up with her, I would hear about all her amazing friends and big nights out. But I consistently kept hearing about this one great guy. He was one of her closest friends, and I was so thrilled that she found someone so special, someone that would look out for her, take care of her if anything happened because I wasn't there. Every time I was supposed to drive up and visit, and finally meet all these people that she kept saying I would absolutely love, something would come up. I either couldn't get away from training, or I was struggling under pressure from my coach, my professors, my peers.... So it went on like this for years until eventually this friend turned into someone she thought of as more than that. Anyone will tell you that moment when you realize you have feelings for a friend. Your life turns to absolute hell. The little gestures, the conversations, the body language—all of a sudden, you take it as something more, as a sign. A week ago you wouldn't have thought anything of his hand on your back or that little smile he shot you from across the table while you were studying. But today, those little things pull you in slowly, make your heart jump a little bit. It takes a while, but after keeping these feelings locked up, a secret, you have to tell someone. That person is usually one of your closest friends, and I couldn't believe that after three years of university, I had never met him. I had seen some pictures, and knew his face, but had no idea what he was like, his personality, his values, or if I would approve. Was he good enough for her? I was so protective. She is the kind of girl that gives so much of herself to everyone around her, and I never wanted anyone taking advantage of that. When you're young and in this new world, you'll do anything to fit in. I had my sport roots to keep me grounded, but I worried about my girls out there. This guy sounded different though, just from the way she spoke about him. I envied her, and had never felt that way about someone.

It takes so much courage to put yourself out there, to put your pride on the line. You run the conversation over and over in your mind, the exact words you're going to say, how you're going to initiate it. You can close your eyes or walk through the motions thinking that if everything goes according to plan, at the end of it all, it will all have been worth it. You see the other person sitting across from you, and feel the colour rushing to your cheeks with the heat creeping up your neck as you imagine their facial expressions, the pounding of your chest drowning out all other sounds. You shake off the nerves though because you picture them falling into your arms afterwards, the perfect kiss, the fairytale ending. I always wanted to believe that if you felt so strongly about someone, that once you proved to them how real it was to you, they would automatically feel the same way. This must be the definition of naivety. Before I experienced the crushing disappointment of my own heartbreak, I was completely oblivious.

But this once perfect guy we had all heard about for so long was the guy I was always afraid she'd find: the one that hurt her. His name became one that I didn't bring up at all after that, and he was slowly phased out of our conversations. As easy as that, he was gone, temporarily erased. Life does go on, even when you think it won't. And hers did. She got through it, moved on, and ended up falling in love with one of the greatest guys I know, all before graduation. But there are moments of vulnerability and loneliness where you can't help but feel horrible, rejected, alone. Every time you see that person that caused it all, you can't help but feel a little something, whether its anger, sadness or loneliness. Until the healing process is complete, they will always have some sort of affect on you. The fact that they were all friends with the same people at university didn't really help, and I remember thinking to myself how hard that would be for her, the constant reminder of him, of his face every day. They would have to be friends.

And then one fateful day I finally met him, the infamous former best friend. The one I call Dave. It was New Years Eve, and she brought him to my house with a few friends in the early hours of the morning. He looked different in person, but I would recognize that face anywhere. Even before I knew him, I had this instant attraction to the one person that was strictly off limits to all of us. Of course that would happen to me. "Stop it!" I screamed to myself, but it was too late. The hair stood up on the back of my neck as he leaned in closer to look over my shoulder, placing his hand on my skin, making fun of my music selection. It only lasted a second, but I can still remember the rush that shot up my spine from his touch. I wanted to turn around and throw my arms around him, pull him close, but I would never have acted on it.

There we were, and I have never felt more awkward. It was 4 a.m., the night was coming to an end, and for some reason the remaining group of us was sitting there talking about gymnastics. This was not the first and definitely not the last conversation I would have with someone where I had to defend what I did. Being the strong, stubborn one, I challenged one of our friends to come watch me train if he didn't think it was so hard. Four hours every morning, be there. Dave sat there silently, half asleep with my best friend leaning on his shoulder. I didn't even think he heard us. They all left shortly after that to go home, and I curled up under the covers, waking up the next morning having forgotten the entire conversation.

I pushed Dave from my mind as best as I could the next few days, and over the holidays it wasn't hard to find distractions. They were everywhere with everyone getting ready to go back to school and trying to spend every last second with each other before saying goodbye. I showed up at training like normal a few days later. There I was all in black, ripped tights, hair in a messy bun, sweaty strands falling in front of my eyes. I felt like I had let my body take over that day, and it wouldn't stop. I was working on a new piece of choreography, and was giving it my all when my teammate grabbed my attention from across the gym and mouthed, "Who's that?" while looking up to the second floor viewing windows. I had no idea what she was talking about, and whipped around expecting another gymnast or someone connected with the sport. And there he was. My mouth hit the floor. Dave. Literally, besides my mom, no one has ever come to watch me train. Not one friend has shown up to see me over the years. I was so completely shocked, my face turned bright red. All I could do was blush and laugh. He stayed for at least an hour watching us train, and I've never pushed myself so hard. My legs found this new strength somewhere, and the show off in me was having a field day. He wanted to see me in action, and he was going to get it. I couldn't believe he actually came, and a part of me was so happy I had to control my facial expressions as the other part was analyzing the whole situation. He had overheard my conversation that night. Was it just a joke? My brain was going a million miles per minute, but all I knew is that this was the day I stopped trying to forget him. No one had ever gone out of their way for me like that, and so obviously shown interest in me. He didn't wait till I finished practice, and left without saying goodbye, leaving me with this disappointed feeling in my stomach. I had to talk to him even though I knew how much trouble it was going to get me into it. But I couldn't help it.

I didn't know what else to do but find a way to contact him. We fell into a rhythm after that, and continued to talk secretly. I didn't let it become a big enough deal to tell my girlfriends, or anyone for that matter. But I was ashamed that I was going behind my best friend's back and could hurt her. The next couple of months were such a painful, challenging time that I realized how fortunate I was to have him in my life. We never saw each other in person, but had the rare opportunity to really get to know each other by talking every day. We were able to skip all the awkward dates and clichéd moments. He saw the real me.

2008 was supposed to be THE year of my life, but it was actually the year that changed me the most. I made sure to guard my feelings around Dave, and told myself not to get caught up in something that wasn't real. I made myself believe that he was just interested in my life as an Olympic gymnast jet-setter, in school, and living in Spain and Toronto. Clearly, what I did was more intriguing than who I actually was. All I knew was that every time I would see his name in my inbox, my face lit up. But I fought it. Months passed by like this, talking about anything and everything. With him, I could be the goofball that I actually am. I could stop being so serious all the time and let him de-stress me, and he could make me laugh like no one else. I would anxiously wait for my phone to light up with a message from him, my heart racing. It was the fall of 2008 after I had survived the Olympic experience, flipped my entire world upside down by retiring, and coming back home when I knew that I had fallen for him. It was irrational and stupid to think this when I hadn't seen him since that New

Years Eve almost a year ago. But there it was, it was true. I was so conflicted that I could feel the tug and pull inside me. I had been strung along for so long by the other one over the last couple of months, the only other guy who I had cared about, that I was mentally exhausted. I knew I had to walk away from the past and face my future, and Dave was it: my future. I wasn't sure how I was going to pull it off, I didn't know if it was right, but I didn't care. I had to see him. He was my little secret, and the extra rush of it being so forbidden made not seeing him even more excruciating. I wasn't sure what was going to happen, but I wasn't going any longer without seeing his face.

And then we finally got our chance.

I can't quite explain what it feels like to be getting ready for a first date when you've been talking to the person for over a year. He knew more about me than most guys ever have, and I was nervous. I spent way too long in the mirror, changed a million times, and ended up wearing the first thing I tried on an hour before. My stomach was in a knot and I couldn't stop fidgeting. I had no idea what was wrong with me. It was just dinner. Not like I had never been on one of these things before. But I was utterly and completely freaking out. I sat on my bed fully dressed in my coat for a good twenty minutes, getting too hot, taking it off, walking around then putting it back on and sitting on the bed again. Glancing at my phone waiting for that red light to flash, my heart was racing a mile a minute with anxiety. I know you all do it too: pick up your phone and check it every two seconds thinking that, miraculously in those few moments, something had changed or you had missed the message somehow. No, you're just crazy. So here I am, all ready to go, and the extremely confident girl had lost her nerve. He waited just long enough for me to start dreaming up all these scenarios in my head that he wasn't coming, that I was going to be stood up, and I'd get a message that he had to cancel as something came up and I was the idiot that was waiting for him. Before I got too completely ahead of myself, there was that red light. My breathing returned back to normal. There he was. I jumped up and checked myself out one more time before I fled the room all bundled up for the cold November night. He smiled at me when we locked eyes, and I stopped short, waiting for him to come to me. He swaggered towards me, that half cocky half nervous kind of walk, reached out and gave me a hug. We stood there and all I could think was that it felt like I had known this boy my whole life. From afar it probably looked like an awkward date or maybe even two old friends meeting for a drink. But it was so much more than that. We were playing our own secret little game, slowly wandering the downtown streets towards the restaurant, finally in person. He took me to this beautiful Italian spot right in the heart of the market, crowded but intimate. I knew this was too good to be true, but I decided to just forget about that for the night. Live in the moment, enjoy the forbidden, soak in the thrill of being there with him right then. So I did. We talked for what felt like hours, both hooked, and we knew it. Fighting the urge, we were waiting to cross the street after we had to leave the restaurant before they kicked us out, and he enveloped me into his arms. Every inch of my body wanted to press my lips against his, but I couldn't do it. His forehead rested on mine, our noses touched ever so slightly. I can't explain it, it was as if we had both fallen for each other a year ago and had been waiting for this moment, letting it build up slowly for twelve long months. I could feel his smile with my eyes closed, the tension, the resistance. We weren't supposed to be doing this; we weren't even supposed to be talking. In my mind, this was the lowest of the low, but all I knew was that I didn't want to let him go that night.

I can't remember who moved closer first, but we stayed up all night just wrapped in each other's arms. We didn't need words. It was so pure, so real. I like to think he was under my spell, but I was under his. I closed my eyes, entangled with him, and a fear washed over me. I was scared that I would wake up and this would be lost forever. I drew him closer, and taking a deep breath, I opened my eyes and took a good look at him, those eyes on me like I was the only girl in the world. I wanted to remember this moment because somewhere inside me I had a feeling that things would never be this uncomplicated ever again. And I was right.

If I could tell my old self one thing, stop time and travel back, I would make myself confess immediately. Secrets between best friends only get harder to keep and more hurtful the longer you keep them inside. If things were different, maybe they wouldn't have worked out anyways and I would have lost the one person that has stuck by my side my whole life. I was scared of losing her. I wasn't ready to grow up. I hadn't put my past behind me, and I was still terrified to commit to someone and let them in. I would've hurt him more and I knew that. I wasn't ready. I tried to date him like a normal relationship, but it was getting so serious so fast. Too fast. I didn't know what to do, so I did the only thing I knew how to do. Push away.

My indecisiveness, guilt and fear ultimately killed what we had. I would pull away from him when all he wanted to do was hold me. I wriggled my hand out of his when he was just trying to hold on to me. I had it in my mind that this was so wrong, so forbidden that I would lose all my friends if they found out. I would lose my best friend forever. I pushed him to a point where he couldn't do it anymore. He wanted it to be real. It was more than a game to him. But I couldn't give him what he wanted. So I gave him the out.

We didn't speak for months, but I couldn't get him off my mind. I didn't want to make the same mistake I had before, and I made sure we eventually found our way back to each other. Even after all the time that had passed, it was just as it was before. There were days when I thought we were so perfect. I could be myself, and he challenged me. He was so positive about everything that it rubbed off on me, and I am so grateful for that. I come down so hard on myself for everything. I always think I'm not good enough, no matter how much work I do or what I accomplish, thinking I could do more. I'm guarded and unsure of myself sometimes; but he gave me great advice and an open mind. I could count on him for that always, regardless if we were in a good place or not. He always had my best interests at heart, and I ended up trusting him completely, which I never thought I could again. Dave would take care of me even when he didn't have time, let me take him with me on whatever crazy idea I had that day: a last-minute over-the-border road trip or black-tie gala. He saw right through my act. He saw me.

Our lives never seemed to sync like they once did before though, and that year we were so on and off because we both travelled so much. "Ms. Independent," he used to call me. The strain of it all being secret, a lie, was constantly weighing down on us. Whenever we could see each other, we would, but it got harder and harder to justify how we could go on like this. As much as it hurt, we let each other go. I tried to move on, but was miserable. We were both so conflicted and confused then, but we couldn't stay away. He was so hot and cold that I never knew if he missed me or just the idea of me, the connection we had that we couldn't deny, and still can't. It was crazy, but something in my gut told me to hold on. Even though he was turning cold towards me, looking at me like I was just another girl now, we began to see each other casually again, here and there. I started hoping for that Dave that used to try and grab my hand along busy streets; long for the guy who couldn't wait to see me. The Dave that slow danced with me in my kitchen, my arms draped around his neck, humming the song, our song. I'm yours. But things had changed and I so desperately tried to not see it. We had somehow switched roles along the way, and all of a sudden he was the one that wouldn't let emotions get in the way; and I was the one pushing for us to be together for real this time. Something inside kept telling me it wasn't over. I was ready to learn from my mistakes.

I couldn't hold back any longer, broke my stubbornness and picked up the phone. That late night, I sat on my bed in the pitch dark with the lights of Dundas Square glaring into my bedroom from my balcony door, and I finally had the conversation I was dreading. That one that you know is coming, but you can't bear to live through. From the bits and pieces I got from it as I zoned in and out of the conversation, completely in shock that it was ending this way—I understood just how much I had hurt him. I was never going to be anything more than a girl he kept at arm's length now.

That feeling he once had had faded, and I don't think he would ever look at me in the same way again. To hear those words broke my heart. He had flipped a switch, shut off a part of himself to me because I would always be the girl that had pushed him away. I hung up and silently let out tears I thought I had gotten rid of years ago. The next few months are always difficult, but you get through them as best you can. I turned that corner out of his sight for the last time. It took all I had in me to keep my head up, and I lost myself. You reminisce about those great pieces of time that you spent together, and you get a dull ache in your chest when you hear a song that reminds you of them; but you survive. You pick yourself up and know you have to move on.

Life is definitely not a movie, that picture-perfect love story that we have come to know. Love doesn't always happen. The boy doesn't always get the girl, and vice versa. People settle or don't let themselves fall. They don't always feel the same way that you do.

It would have been the cowardly thing to forget that it had ever happened and grow older with my best friend with this secret lurking somewhere in the shadows. I knew that eventually she would find out in her own way, and for us to get closer, I had to come clean. She is the one person I never thought I could lie to, and I couldn't do it anymore. What I couldn't do for two years, I did within 24 hours of making up my mind. The timing was finally right, and I was now mature enough and secure with myself and our relationship to give her the respect she deserved. My stomach was in knots as I sat her down and prepared myself for the absolute worst. Hurting her was the last thing I wanted to do. I was terrified. To an outsider, the tiny, beautiful girl sitting in front of me would never be capable of lunging across the table for my neck. But my imagination was running wild. I could barely look her in the eyes as I told her, sick to my stomach. I waited for her to storm out, but she didn't.

We get so caught up in the past and with things that once seemed life ending, that we forget how much we've grown and how far we've come from that point. I didn't see it until then. I didn't give my best friend the credit she deserved. I didn't give her the benefit of the doubt that, yes, maybe she just did want me to be happy. Drama and scandals and gossip had surrounded my young adulthood, and I couldn't open my eyes wide enough to see that we're past all that. I sat across from her with an open heart for the first time in a long time, and thought I would lose her. I was stupid to think that she would go anywhere as she'd been there for me through everything. And believe me, I didn't have the typical problems that most teenagers go through. But she never ran like so many others. I wish I had realized we were grownups long before I did, before I gave up on him, before I hurt him; but maybe I wasn't ready to see it then. We sat there like two idiots crying in public, but we have never been closer. She has seen me struggle with finding myself and reaching my potential since I was a little girl, and she would be by my side to get me through this.

I woke up the next morning and felt like a new person. There were so many incredible things in my life that I was and am fortunate and grateful to have. Remember that strong and confident young woman who would never let anyone stand in her way? She's still in there. If we let people think we're undeserving or not good enough, we've let them win. Don't let anyone get you down because in the end it's not worth it. Look around you and appreciate the beauty you have in your life, the things that make you happy every day. Tell the people in your life today that you love them, and thank them for being there for you. No matter how frustrated or hurt you are, life goes on, and the people that are closest to you will never leave your side.

I was finally back to normal, with a refreshed outlook on my life and my relationships, ready to take anything on. That sense of empowerment is so powerful, you feel on top of the world. A rush comes over you, coursing throughout your body, putting a confident smile on your face as you strut down the street like it's a catwalk, or hit the treadmill faster than normal. I stopped checking my phone, I stopped caring. I thought you were finally out of my head, my dreams. That's until we ran into each other.

You didn't see me at first. The bar was dark, crowded, and full of pretty young things everywhere. I stopped in to see a friend, and there I was dressed down, leather jacket and jeans amid all the hot flesh in tight, short dresses. The vodka was flowing when I got there. The music pounded, and I let myself seep into the scene and have a good time. I found my girlfriend, and we danced and laughed until I saw you. But the Dave that was there that night was a Dave that I have never seen before. You were drinking way too much, way too fast, with girls draped all over you, loving it. To see your hands all over them, the corporate arrogance and old boys club you were with was enough to make me think I didn't really know who you were after all.

As I turned around to jet out, refusing to let you see me so upset, I ran right smack into you. You stopped short and took a startled step back, so confused as to why I was standing there in front of you. I could barely look at you, it was so hard. Every question you asked I gave the shortest answer I could think of. You effortlessly put your hand in mine, an act that felt so natural I didn't think anything of it. You interlaced your fingers with mine, tightening your grip and pulling me close with our hands behind my back now, your lips searching for mine. But I had to turn away. You whispered in my ear. I squeezed my eyes shut, stuck in this moment, praying that when I opened them again it would be a year ago. But it wasn't. I opened them to a crowded bar with a year of heartache wedged in between us, and a blonde in a red dress on your arm. I couldn't look back once I let go.

It makes me sad how much things change. Over the last year, day by day, a little bit more poison seeped into us. I had to accept that he didn't want me anymore. It was one of the hardest things I've had to face. Reality does hurt. There are people that pick up and move halfway around the world, walk away from their jobs, their families, and drop everything to sacrifice it all for that one person. That's the kind of person you want to be with, someone who thinks you're worth it. Whether he wanted to or not, he made me feel that I'm not worth the chance, not worth the aggravation. He thought we fought more than we got along, but that wasn't it at all. He got it wrong. I just asked for a chance, for a shot to make it right, but he wouldn't give it to me. I'm still not sure why. I would have given him everything.

There are days when I look back on my love life and think that maybe if I was different, if I had been softer, less of a whirlwind, maybe I would have had my happy ending. But my life is this way because of who I am. You should never have to change who you are or compromise what makes you, you, for someone else. Even if that means you're alone. I thought Dave was different, I thought that he would see that this didn't come around every day. Maybe now that I'm ready for something real, he realized he never actually was. Thank you for coming into my life. I know it was for a reason. You made me feel something that I never thought I could again. You ended up hurting me, but instead of closing myself off, it opened me up; and I believe it now more than ever before that we're both debatably broken in such an imperfect perfect way. And I can live with that.

Chapter 13: We Were Warriors

"If the mother falls, the entire family falls." Halfway around the world, I heard this on the streets of Delhi, India, and it made me think of my mother.

My mother always told me I would never understand what it felt like to care so much about a person, to worry about them every minute of every day, to love the way a mother does. I rolled my eyes every time she said it, secretly thinking that she was just the way she was because she had me as a daughter. I never denied I was a handful, never denied that I wasn't difficult. I've known since I was a little girl that she had to put up with more than she probably ever thought possible. But I also knew that every day was unpredictable, and that it was an unbelievable adventure for both of us.

I was devious and mischievous when I was younger, and she always said I had this look in my eyes like I knew I was going to do something bad, and would do it anyways. I would make her laugh so hard that her insides ached. We had so much fun together. I loved to play. Everything was a joke, everything could be fun. There are many photos of me holding on to her hand, clinging to her leg. Both Victoria and I couldn't live without her. She is our mom, and I don't think I understood how much that actually meant then, but I knew that she laid down the law and that she was there by my side giving me ginger ale and wrapping me up in blankets when I was sick. She would sing to me softly when I couldn't sleep, and she let me dress myself, even if that meant two different socks. She fed us and, most importantly to me, played with us. She was just like a kid, dressing up on Halloween, running around the backyard with us or playing board games. She will always be the Scrabble Queen. She did it all. When I think of my childhood, I think of her. She made sure we all got from point A to point Z, never once complaining, never once letting us see how tired she may have been. She is a fighter, and I don't think we ever gave her credit for it.

When my dad had his heart attack, I didn't know what was going on. I was waiting at the top of the stairs for him as usual, but he was working late that night. Something was different. I can only imagine the scene because I was fast asleep when it happened. He dropped his briefcase and looked up. He was green. He called out her name: "Marisa". From their bedroom, she ran to him in milliseconds as if she had known that this was going to happen. She was so scared. The next few minutes were all a blur, but the blaring sirens of the ambulance brought her back to life. To be with my dad as he was whisked away by strangers, men in full gear, she must have been so confused and terrified. Victoria and I stayed with our neighbours, our second family. She told us, "Daddy was going to be fine. He just had to stay in the hospital". Life resumed as normal, but hers didn't. She kept our family together, put her own feelings aside to keep us happy, and the stress ate her alive. Pounds melted off her, but she never once crumbled. So selfless, I can only hope to find a love that would make me so selfless like that one day. She raised two beautiful daughters and brought a man back to life, from the war, a heart attack, and a lifetime of trying to prove himself. She cared for us all, and I don't think she took the time to care for herself.

She always called me her "little monkey," climbing on everything, crawling all over the place and creating my own little world wherever I went. I would escape from her in the department stores and love to hide among the racks of clothing. I think that's why she eventually put me on a leash. I would pick things up with my toes and cling to my dad's legs. I was a monkey. Small and agile, I would do the unthinkable. One day I climbed onto Victoria's desk and tried to get to the top of her bookshelf. She heard the crash from the kitchen downstairs and knew it was me, running upstairs screaming my name, and bursting into Victoria's room to find the bookshelf collapsed on the floor. For a second I'm sure she thought I had been crushed, only to see my little head poke out of the triangle of space it had left balancing on the overturned desk, with my wide grin, laughing. I made her worry every day as she never knew what I was going to do. I'm surprised she didn't tie me to a chair some days, strap me in and never let me out of her sight. I thank her for giving me the freedom to make my own mistakes, to let go of my hand and watch me try and climb mountains.

My mother has such a giving nature that she is always the first person to help you when you're hurting. My sister confided in her very early on, while I kept to myself, quiet and private, not willing to share the intimate details of my life like Victoria. I wish I could open up to my mom like she can, that I was more open, more of a best friend. But even though for so many years I kept everything inside, if I ever wanted help, I would go to her. If I couldn't do it alone and I needed someone, she was there. I have never been one to show her how much I love her, how much she means to me, but my love for her is indescribable. I can be so cold to her, so unforgiving, so over the line. But I know she can take it because she'll always love me. I took so much of my frustration and anger out on her when I couldn't yell or scream in the gym, or say things to people that I always wanted to say. Instead, she was my punching bag. I worry about being the person she didn't want me to become. I would never want her to think that because of a choice she and my father let me live out, that I'm damaged, broken. She gave me my dream. She let me make the choice. There aren't too many mothers out there that have the strength to watch their daughter in pain for days, weeks or months on end. There aren't too many mothers that can still support a decision that would take their child on a journey in which they may never come home as the same person. But she did. She stood strong for years, trying so desperately to help me when she knew I needed it. She gave me everything in the world, but I didn't want to take it. I tried to be so tough, to do it all on my own. But when I look back on my career, I know I should have leaned on her when she was right there. I should have taken her hand. So many nights I cried to her, and would come home in a rage with no one else to load it off on. She was the only one there, day in and day out. I led a double life, keeping up this picture-perfect image of myself on the outside as there was no room to scream, vent or explode. Only with her, behind closed doors, could I do it. I needed to release all the anger I had inside of me, to be rude and talk back. I can never apologize enough for putting her through that. There were days when I made her cry and she would sit at the kitchen table with her head in her hands, and the tears would stream down her cheeks. I did that. I said the things you're not supposed to say, things that I never even meant. I was nasty and hurtful. Every time I was told I was fat or not good enough, every time I had let myself down in the gym—she was my release. And yet she never stopped loving me. She tried to understand me and where all of it was coming from, but I could never tell her. I now realize that even though she won't ever understand what I was going through, she could feel it. Every torn ligament or twisted ankle burned a hole in her chest. Each setback or disappointment ripped at her seams. Things weren't always like that, and this new life of mine has put it all behind us; but we shared a part of our lives that neither one of us will ever forget: endless memories that have brought us closer than ever. If she was a different person, I may have never found the strength inside of me to become an Olympian. She made me believe I could do anything.

I hope she sees herself in me. I am more like her than I like to think, and I keep her university student card on my desk next to mine. It is scary how alike we look, that pitch-black, long and thick hair; the smirk, no teeth. She was silent like me once, private. She kept things from her mother, and didn't want to be smothered. We're the same and she knows it, except she doesn't smother me. It only feels like she does sometimes. I need my space, and will only let her in when I want to, not because she wants me to. I hope that when my mother looks at me, she knows she's raised a daughter who understands where she came from, and who she is. That she understands the meaning of family and our heritage. That she values her mother. Because I do.

Watching my parents over the years has taught me what love really is. I question whether it even exists anymore, their kind of love, the kind of love that never dies. It's something I rarely see anymore. Two people who have promised to spend their entire lives together, and that have stood by it. They are by no means perfect, but they respect each other, and have sacrificed. They've helped each other through incredibly hard times. Together they're one. They have both kept this family together, and have been different things to my sister and me. They can fight and yell, but it is out of love not hate. They always apologize to each other, and never go to bed angry. I love seeing the little private moments no one is meant to see, like his hand on her back, a kiss on the cheek as she's making dinner, and his hand on hers when they're watching TV. Their love is still so strong. It is magical. They met so young, and my mom's family adopted him as if he was one of their own. They became his family even though he was so much older. She was so sure, and I can't wait to find that feeling, to know what that's like. They have set the bar so incredibly high that I can't imagine finding a man who could make me feel so safe, so secure, so in love like my father is with her. It is truly incredible how they both know when to speak their mind, when to be silent, and when to be strong. They keep each other calm when the world doesn't seem to stop spinning, and the struggles my career put them through never weighed on the love that they had for each other.

Being the parent of an elite athlete, especially an individual athlete who's not part of a team where the highs and lows are shared and experienced together, is harder than my mother could have imagined. All the expectations were on me, alone; and so she was also alone. There were other parents to share in the journey, and she made some lifetime friends along the way. But no matter what, it was just me and her, in the car, at physio, in hotel rooms, on a plane, singing, laughing, celebrating, crying together and crying alone. She had to hold back the tears for me so many times.

She wasn't there to be my coach and tell me what I was doing right or wrong. She was there to be my support system and a shoulder to lean on. If I had a bad day, her job was to value my performance and love me unconditionally. She was there to make sure that life outside of rhythmic gymnastics went as smoothly as possible so that I could still go to school, get good grades, and do what I loved. When I would go off on a journey, she would always tell me not to forget to have some fun too.

My mom knew how difficult all the long training camps were for me, all the back-to-back trips that took me far away from home. She couldn't be there with me, even though she would have wanted to. So she would write me letters to take away with me that made it easier to survive even the darkest of days. I would wait until I touched down in some remote airport in a city thousands of miles away from home before I opened them. I would open them with caution, and read every word slowly. My family photos gave me hope that there were people waiting for me back home who loved me with every part of their being. They were people who believed in me no matter what. I would read her beautiful words over and over, every day, every night. When I was alone in my head, I would think of her. She knew that I was going to be tested wherever I was, and she knew that I was putting it out on the line every time I flew off to compete or train. It was all so important, every move I made, how I carried myself. Her cursive writing would be hard to read sometimes, but I got used to it. She made me so proud to be who I was, without ever feeling bad for my success or the ambition that drove me out of bed in the morning. She said all the things I didn't want to hear in front of friends or family, as I never wanted to be in the spotlight like that. But deep down she knew how important it was for me to hear it, to celebrate in my own way what I had accomplished, and what I was going to do. It secretly made getting through the endless hours of training and injuries so much easier. I remember sitting on the floor, locked in the bathroom of my apartment in Moscow that I shared with twelve to fifteen Russian gymnasts. There were six of us in a room with bunk beds, and a woman who cleaned and cooked for us, controlling all the portions. I was alone, the only Canadian, and the training was the hardest I've ever endured in my life. My mom sent me a few letters to open throughout the training camp and help me through. Locking the bathroom door behind me was the only time I could get any alone time, any peace and quiet without the constant talk of gymnastics or gossiping in a language I didn't understand. I felt so alone, but with her writing in my hands I would find the strength to get up the next day and do it all again. I would sit there on the floor and run the water so the others would give up trying to get in, and would leave me be. When I couldn't breathe, she gave me air.

Being the parent of a champion when you also have another child, is twice as hard. My mom would come away with me sometimes, or be so extremely involved in the business of the sport that it would take up most of her time. She acted as my agent and a liaison with the Ontario and Canadian gymnastics organizations. They had to pass everything by her when I was younger, and she was constantly driving me to the gym after school, and would run home, make dinner for Victoria, and drive back again. She had to juggle her time between both of us, but there was no comparison. I can only hope Victoria knows what she means to mom and what she contributed by allowing her to support me the way she did. When we all went to the Olympics, there was no doubt that Victoria was also coming to the big show. It was to be the end of an era for us all. I won't ever be able to tell her what it felt like to walk out into the Olympic arena and see her face in the stands. I looked over my shoulder and there was Victoria, holding the Canadian flag, screaming and jumping on her feet in a "Team Alex" t-shirt. My mom stood there with the people I love the most in the world: my sister, father, aunt and uncle. The emotions running through my body were indescribable. Everything we had worked for, sacrificed, fought over, the furniture they could never buy, and the vacations we couldn't go on, all flashed before my eyes. She had never looked happier, more proud. Something inside me was screaming, but all I could do was smile. The pressure hit me in the face and knocked me over before I could soak in this feat. When I got off the plane in China, stepped foot in the athlete village and was handed an accreditation telling the world I was an Olympic athlete—I could then scream it at the top of my lungs. I felt like I was flying, and those few precious minutes I walked around the competition floor holding the Canadian flag high, every step brought me higher. It felt like my mom was there beside me, and she deserved to be. The pain that had been on my mind for months, the agony that 2008 brought when it was supposed to be the best year of my life—was gone. To have her there to celebrate with me meant more than whatever I did out there on the floor in front of the judges. Having her there to witness our life work, made me realize that with my family behind me, no one could ever say I wasn't good enough ever again. No one could tell me I couldn't do anything I put my mind to.

When I first started gymnastics, she thought I was just having fun, but behind my big smile and bundle of energy was a very competitive little girl. At eight years old, when I won that first medal, she knew this was going to be a part of our lives for a very long time. It takes a certain personality to be successful in sport. It means hours and hours training in the gym every day, sometimes alone, having to look a certain way, giving up social activities, having to prove yourself time and again. She couldn't understand it, but knew that I wanted this, and she was going to let me go for it. It meant changing her path in life, and she could say that we should have made some different choices, but I don't believe in looking back. I wanted to go to the Olympics, and I did, so the choices we made worked.

We persisted against the odds. The odds being that this is an Eastern European sport, and to push yourself into the spotlight was very difficult. They are professional athletes with no other life, and so very hard to compete with. But she always told me that

I had that certain something. She never could really explain it, but when I stepped out on the carpet it was as if everyone was watching. She saw me as a born competitor and entertainer, and no one was going to stop me. She loves that I set goals for myself and see them through. And she loves my confidence, looking those judges in the eyes knowing I have to be flawless to get their attention.

As a parent she had to sit back and watch her daughter be coached by very tough, but incredibly talented coaches. It was their job to create a champion. They knew I had the capability to do it, and they trained me to be the very best. She didn't interfere with the coaching, but I know she had private talks with my coach when she didn't like what was happening in the gym. It was very natural and normal for the coaches because this is the way they are accustomed to training. But it was not natural for my mom. Watching someone else make me feel like I wasn't good enough, seeing the hurt in my eyes—it was a pain in her heart. But those days would come and go. I would call her from the gym to tell her when I was having a great day, and I did this to reassure her. I knew she was hurting too, and I think I was trying to protect her. But there are so many things she doesn't know, that I didn't have the strength to break to her. It made her sick to her stomach when I was told I didn't have the right body type to get good scores, or I wasn't working hard enough. She would cringe at the call display if it was my coach calling to tell her I wasn't working well, or asking what I ate. They thought she was an Italian mother stuffing my face with pasta every night. It drove her insane. She was the one that most helped me eat properly. There were those nights I would come home and not want to eat, and there was nothing she could do because no one was harder on me than me. I knew that she would be behind me no matter what I decided, but I was in love with this sport. What could she say to a young woman who had given up so much to be in the gym day after day, being yelled at, and was only good enough when getting the scores they wanted, and looked a certain way? What could she say to this girl who had so much fire, passion and spirit in her? She couldn't take my dreams away.

And then there were the highs, and so many of them. Winning Nationals for so many years; Pan Am Games; setting a record at Commonwealth Games; breaking into the Eastern European bloc at World Championships; and The Olympic Games. All that hard work and training paid off. She will never forget going to Brazil for the IV Continents Championships when I was thirteen, and I had a security guard with me because the fans wanted my autograph. That was only the beginning. Everywhere she went people would tell her how much I meant to them and how their young daughters looked up to me. She never had to teach me to be humble, but I was never one to talk about what I had accomplished. Many people who just met me didn't even know I was an athlete unless they talked to my dad. He would never have given up either. She always said we were warriors.

My mom kept so much inside to allow me to do this thing that I loved so much. Watching me compete made her forget the part of the sport she didn't like, made her fall in love with this sport. She would say you could see the fire and passion in my soul. It was magical.

I don't think she ever realized how much she would miss rhythmic gymnastics when I retired. The withdrawal, the loss. After seventeen years of sport, it was over just like that, with no finality, no goodbyes, nothing. She would never see me compete again, never watch me perform. Her job was over. She kept in touch with friends from the community, and went to competitions, but it wasn't the same. She missed me. She still does. I can never thank her enough for what she sacrificed and endured for me. All she wanted was for me to be happy. She always praises me for being the strong one, unstoppable; but she was the warrior. She has been the fighter all along.

Ti amo.

Chapter 14:
New Beginnings

Twenty-five years have seemed to go by so quickly. I can't believe everything that has come and gone: the people, the trips, my career. Years blur together now, pieces of my life so easily forgotten, memories once so vivid starting to fade. Everyone around me has aged, matured; and we speak, look and feel differently. Priorities have changed, lives have shifted.

I sit at my kitchen table, the same table I would come home to after a long day at practice and do my homework on. The table that I sat across from the first boy I brought home, playing with his hands, hidden out of sight with its protection. The chairs that my friends would sit on for hours, talking until the candles burned out and our glasses were empty. The breaking of bread, the peace-making with my coach and my parents. The tears that hit the hard, cold marble. I now watch the people around me from this very spot, this familiar place; and my family moves from room to room, as I go unnoticed. My grandma is so quiet now, she sips her wine slower, holds her hugs longer. Nothing is taken for granted. My parents come home a little earlier from a night out, stay in more, soak up the time they have together, enjoy travelling, and talk about the future without our house. It's lonely for my mother. My big sister is getting married. Wedding plans, dreams for their children and their life together. They are their own family now. It is the start of their own traditions, their own special memories without us, without me.

A selfish piece of me wants everything to stay the same, make time stop and keep us all cozy and loud under this roof. Sunday dinners at the dining room table, movie nights on our big suede couches, my sister's room across from mine littered with memories of our childhood. For years I lived out of a suitcase, travelled the world, had to make new friends, switch schools, and try and fit in over and again. But the one thing I could always count on was this house and my family in it. With my world always seeming to be falling apart, these walls could block out the pressure, the noise; and I could escape. I felt safe. I was home.

It's bittersweet to see us all go down different paths now, new phases of life, of discovery. I always knew this day would come, but I'm not as ready for it as I thought I would be. I walk down these halls, run my fingertips along the pictures, flashes of my former life, our former life. I step foot into a room that I don't even recognize anymore, my once coveted hideout, my safe haven. But I've outgrown it. The hundreds of medals that hang from the walls, trophies that adorn the shelves, flags and mementos from trips around the world—they stare back at me. Images of my teammates and I at different ages in front of historical icons and beautiful skylines. It's hard to even remember what being that girl was like.

When I retired from rhythmic gymnastics at twenty-one, I didn't realize that I would also lose a part of who I was as well. But I was so ready to be done, to heal my body, to relax, and for once not worry about letting someone down, and about fitting a mould I was never meant to fit. I wanted to be a university student like my friends, study, stay up late. I was ready to retire, I knew that, but I never thought it would make me feel the way it did. I would never say my sport was my whole life, but I would be lying if I said that all my goals, my dreams and my decisions growing up weren't affected by it. It touched all of our lives, every person that came into my life—for good or bad.

All of a sudden I wasn't the gymnast anymore. I wasn't the centre of attention. Your sport, your community: it moves on without you. Like everything else, there was a new national champion, a new girl to replace me. I was scared that I would be forgotten, a distant memory, some girl who used to be amazing. The fear of being washed up was creeping into my subconscious. There was no team of people around me anymore, helping me get the best out of myself, watching what I ate, mending my wounds, training me in the gym. Choreographers and coaches didn't come around to see how I was doing, how they could help me improve. I seemed to have fallen off the face of the earth.

I came home from the Olympics battered, bruised and confused. For the last competition of my life, I thought I would feel elated. I thought that no matter what, I would feel satisfied, happy. But all I could feel was this emptiness inside me. It was really all over. My coach went back to Spain. I came home to Toronto to a full-time university schedule. Life resumed as normal. The buzz over the Olympics died down, and Team Canada had done well. No one complained. We all ended on such an incredible high, so to come home to such a low threw me into shock. It felt as if I was on vacation, and I would be back in the gym in a few weeks. But I wouldn't be. There was no goodbye. No time for thank yous. No nothing. One day I was five-time Canadian National Champion, and the next I was just Alex. Your success and past accomplishments always stay with you, and the hope that you'll be remembered for your passion, your strength, your ability to break boundaries, is always there. That will never go away. But it's not your life anymore. You change, you grow up, and you move on.

I came home and took down all my medals, put my trophies in boxes, and removed the pictures from my walls. My parents watched, horrified that I would want to hide it all away. It wasn't because I wasn't proud of myself, I was. I couldn't bear to look at it, the memories, what I had given up. I couldn't let it define me or else I would lose myself. After time, things slowly started to come out of their hiding place, and I've begun talking about my career, about what I have done. I would rarely speak of it before, and let my friends do the talking, too humble, too scared to let it take over me. There was a woman in there that could stand on her own without being an Olympian. She was strong and brave, ambitious and determined. Going to the Olympics didn't prove that, it was always there inside of me.

Looking back, I have no regrets. I know that everything happened for a reason even if I had thought it was unfair. I wish I could have believed in myself more when I was younger. I wish I had seen that all I had to do was get out of my own way sometimes and things may have been easier. I was so tough and so guarded that I fought with everyone, every step of the way. I thrived on it even when it was self-destructing. As much as I wanted to blame my coach, my mother, or whomever for things not going right in my life, I was the difficult one most of the time. I see that now. I was defensive and angry after too many years of being in the shadows and believing I was inadequate. It made me stubborn, hard. I was a fighter and I'll always be one, but as much as it was that thing inside me that brought out my passion, my fire on the carpet could be my worst enemy. I apologize for those that got caught in the crossfire, to all the nights my coach couldn't sleep and my mother cried. I'm sorry. As much as I will never forget things that were done to me or said over the years in the gym, there is no one to blame for the bumps we hit in the road. All I can do is own up to my mistakes and faults, and learn from them. My mother always told me I could only control myself and nothing else. I couldn't control other people, other gymnasts, other judges. I couldn't control the weather that day or the moods that my teammates were in, but I could choose to focus only on me and my performance. I could make a change, make a difference in how I spoke, the attitude I maintained. I could be the light among all the darkness. I was beautiful no matter what anyone said. And I tried to never forget that.

My teammates were my family, and for us all to have gone our separate ways now saddens me. We always said we would be there for each other. They saw my pain, my triumphs, the real me. We loved and hated each other; hoped for the best and held nothing back. Without a word they understood me and what I was going through because we were there living it. They were all fighters, and there is nothing like being on a team like that. I now sit at my desk in an office with incredible co-workers, and we call ourselves a team. But nothing could compare to the team of gymnasts I belonged to. To find a group of people that share every moment of your struggles, to feel what you feel, to push each other in a competitive sport environment—is unlike anything else I have ever known. They stayed up all night with me when I couldn't sleep, and I took care of them when they weren't feeling well on a long haul flight to South America or Asia. We became young women together, learning how to travel the world by ourselves, conquer airports, foreign languages, jet lag and incredible amounts of stress. Some days I long for the whirlwind lifestyle we once had, jetting around the world with one job to do. No matter how bad the hotel or the food, we always found something to smile about. Now that we are all outside the sport looking in, I would hope that they all feel the same way. The secret looks shot across the gym, the support. It taught me how to listen to others, to lead, but follow when I had to. It taught me how to respect others, to learn from them and trust them.

That is why I have always felt so connected to sport. It wasn't the medals, the glory, or even the Olympics. It was the ever-winding road of the unexpected that stole my heart. I could never walk away from it. Even retirement couldn't keep me away, though I tried to let it. I owed everything I ever had to people that supported me, the local clubs that fundraised for me, the young girls that followed my career, and my community of friends and family. I wanted to give back. I wanted to use my experience, my life, to help others. I started coaching, and was elected to a number of boards as an athlete representative for national sport organizations and athlete advocacy groups. I believe strongly in the capability and potential of the Canadian sport system, and devote my time to help make changes to benefit our athletes. Better funding, more resources, more opportunities to develop their potential. I even began judging gymnastics, and as hard as it was at first, it's how I kept one foot in the door to the community, the family I once loved so dearly. I feel at home here, even if it's on the other side of the line in a blue suit scrutinizing the girls whom I once was. I put my life on hold to experience the 2010 Vancouver Olympics on home soil; and I went to India to volunteer for Team Canada and help run the Commonwealth Games. When I graduated from the University of Toronto, I found myself at my first desk job at the Toronto 2015 Pan/Parapan American Games Organizing Committee. My life is truly surrounded by sport, and I wouldn't have it any other way. The value of sport is so powerful, so much more meaningful than people think. It has the ability to bring together a nation, and to unify the world under a common thread. It instills a certain pride in people, inspiring millions. Sport can transform communities, and it can change lives. I know this to be true, because it changed mine.

For so long, all people could see was the athlete in me, but now as I step into a life with my athletic career behind me, I find myself constantly evolving, discovering the woman behind the Olympian, behind sport. I am looking forward to the person I want to become, the person I know I can be. If I've learned anything from my past it's to stop being afraid of letting go, of falling into the unknown, of not being good enough. I'll never be perfect, but it's the imperfections in us that make us unique. You have the world at your fingertips if you want it, but you have to go out and get it. If you fail, try again—never stop trying.

I have learned the hard and cold way that no matter what you look like on the outside, there are people out there that will love you for you. For years I hated myself, and it filled me up inside, a darkness so black that I lost myself. That confident girl was gone. She was suffocating under layers of fake smiles and an insecure gut-wrenching feeling that took over her body. She wasn't Alex anymore. It pains me to see women who are going through what I went through, but are so deep in denial that they can't see that they're killing themselves. Your eyes play tricks on you. That beauty that you don't see, that beauty that we all speak of doesn't exist. Beauty is what you make it to be.

To the two that broke my heart, both so different yet alike. You've given me faith that I could feel something for someone, something so strong I never knew it could exist. I gave that up for me, my career, for what I believed in; and I don't regret it. I tried so hard to run from hurt, worried I would never trust again, but you made me stronger. You taught me to stay true to myself, and even though you hurt me, I know you've helped me grow into the woman I am today: the woman who can open herself to people again, who forgets what heartache feels like, who can fall in love.

I definitely don't have all the answers, but the journey to uncover them makes us who we are. I don't know where I'll be in five, ten, or fifteen years, but I will take everything my life has taught me to help navigate the roads ahead. Live to the fullest, laugh constantly, and love with an open heart. Even though things change or come to an end, you can always find something that drives you and moves you to your very core. I constantly seek that kind of fulfillment, that feeling of absolute certainty that you're exactly where you want to be. Never settle for anything less.

Life is unpredictable, but you have to have hope that you'll find your way. Hope that even when you feel lost, you have enough will inside of you to get out of bed in the morning and hold your head up high. Hope that you can make anything work. Find that kind of hope and don't let it go. It can take you further than you ever dreamed it could.

TIMELINE

2008 • Olympian

       • 5-time Canadian Senior National Champion

       • Pacific Rim Champion

2007 • World Championships, 9th AA, Qualifying for Beijing Olympic Games

       • Pan American Games—3 gold medals

       • Canadian Flag Bearer for the Closing Ceremonies

2006 • Outstanding Female Athlete of the Year—Commonwealth Sports Awards

       • Commonwealth Games Champion

       • Broke a World Record for rhythmic gymnastics by winning 6 gold medals and tying the Games Record for most golds won by a single athlete

       • Canadian Flag Bearer at the Closing Ceremonies

       • Received World-Class Gymnast Award from International Gymnastics Federation

2004 • Pacific Alliance Silver Medalist

2003 • Pan American Games—3 silver and 2 bronze medals

2002 • Pacific Alliance Bronze Medalist

2000 • Junior Pan American Champion

2001 • Portimao International Championships—4 gold medals

       • 2-time Canadian Junior National Champion

       • IV Continents Junior Silver Medalist

1999 • Canadian Novice National Champion

ALEXANDRA ORLANDO is a highly decorated world-class athlete. In her sixteen years dedicated to rhythmic gymnastics, she has been Novice, Junior, and five-time Senior Canadian National Champion. During this time she was Canada's dominant rhythmic gymnast, while earning a reputation as one of the few non-Europeans competing at the sport's highest level.

In 2007 she placed an outstanding ninth place at the 2007 World Rhythmic Gymnastics Championships, qualifying a spot for Canada in the 2008 Beijing Olympic Games. She was the only athlete from all of the Americas to achieve an Olympic berth, and the first Canadian to make a final at a World Championships in twenty-two years.

Just a few months earlier, she won 3 gold medals at the 2007 Pan American Games in Brazil, and was chosen as Canada's flag bearer for the Closing Ceremonies. Alexandra was given the great honour of also carrying Canada's flag at the Closing Ceremonies of the 2006 Commonwealth Games one year earlier, where she won 6 gold medals and broke a world record for her sport. Alexandra was chosen as the 2006 Outstanding Female Athlete of the Year at the Commonwealth Sports Awards held in London, England.

Hundreds of young athletes across Canada look up to Alexandra. She has been an excellent role model and ambassador for sport. Through coaching, speaking engagements, technical skills consultations, self-esteem and motivational workshops, she has helped and inspired many young athletes across a variety of sports.

With over ten years of media training as an elite athlete, Alexandra has made numerous appearances as a keynote speaker and MC for large corporate events. She was also a main spokesperson for the Toronto 2015 Pan/Parapan American Games Bid, consistently speaking with the media and gaining invaluable on-camera experience. Alexandra has done commentary for international rhythmic gymnastics events, and hopes to combine her love of sport and public speaking with a future in broadcasting.

As an active athlete advocate, Alexandra sits on the Canadian Olympic Committee's Women in Sport and Youth and Education

Committees. She is also a mentor for the Canadian Youth Olympic Team that will be competing at the 2010 Youth Olympic Games in Singapore.

Alexandra is an active Right to Play and KidSport Athlete Ambassador, promoting healthier, active living for all.

In 2006, Alexandra co-authored a book about her life and her sport: *Alexandra Orlando in Pursuit of Victory*. From this experience, she has gone on to become a freelance senior writer for CBC and a number of non-profit organizations including the Strength Within Group, empowering young women to make a difference. *Breaking Through My Limits: An Olympian Uncovered* is her second book.

She currently sits on the AthletesCAN Board of Directors as Vice President, and as an Executive Member of the Canadian Olympic Committee's Athletes' Commission. She was formerly the athlete representative on the Gymnastics Canada Board of Directors, and continues to stay heavily involved as an international coach and judge. Alexandra also sat on the Toronto 2015 Pan/Parapan American Games Bid Board of Directors.

Retiring from competitive sport in 2009, Alexandra became a program coordinator at the Institute at Havergal College, and subsequently designed and implemented the Pan/Parapan Am Bid Youth Program. She is currently a Marketing Associate at the Toronto 2015 Organizing Committee, where she continues to thrive in the Canadian sporting community.

Alexandra has the ability to demonstrate, inspire, and teach. Her energy and enthusiasm are infectious, and her love of and support for the athletes' movement across Canada and the world are strong and unwavering. It has been her passion and her dream since she was a young child to play this role, and she performs it so well.

www.alexandraorlando.ca
www.youtube.com/alexandraorlando

Follow Alexandra on Twitter @FreshFromAlex